# Bigger Than
# Little Rock

# Bigger Than Little Rock

BY ROBERT R. BROWN

THE SEABURY PRESS

S·P·C·K

GREENWICH · CONNECTICUT · 1958

© 1958 by The Seabury Press, Incorporated
Library of Congress Catalog Card Number: 58-9226
Design by P. Atkinson Dymock
*Printed in the United States of America*
283-958-C-5

*To the Clergy of Little Rock*

# PREFACE

I am deeply grateful for the assistance of many friends in the preparation of this report. Mr. Gene Fretz of the *Arkansas Gazette* has been especially helpful in providing news accounts and editorials from his paper. The Reverend Joel Pugh, II, has offered invaluable service with the research by finding confirmation of materials that would otherwise have had to be deleted. Mrs. Walter McDonald, Registrar of the Diocese of Arkansas, gathered for me much of the newspaper and magazine materials that served both to refresh my memory and to substantiate some of my arguments. My fellow workers, Bishop Paul E. Martin, Rabbi Ira S. Sanders, the Reverend Aubrey G. Walton, Monsignor James E. O'Connell, and the Reverend Marion A. Boggs have graciously consented to my requests for quotes, as have the Episcopal clergy of Little Rock. To these very good friends, my sincere appreciation.

For comparison and for other viewpoints I am especially indebted to *The Louisville Story* by Omer Carmichael and Weldon James; *The Kingdom Beyond Caste* by Liston Pope; *The Mind of the South* by W. J. Cash; *The Deep South Says 'Never'* by John Bartlow Martin, and *Christian Living* by Stephen F. Bayne, Jr. I commend these volumes to the reader whatever his position may be.

R.R.B.

vii

# CONTENTS

# Bigger Than
# Little Rock

# 1

## WHY?

On October 5, 1955, at Trinity Cathedral in the city of Little Rock, I was ordained and consecrated "into the sacred office of a bishop." Up to the time of my arrival the month before, my personal knowledge of Arkansas and its people had been limited to what I had learned during a brief visit the previous May; and aside from the Rt. Rev. R. Bland Mitchell, I was acquainted with only one clergyman in the entire diocese. For twelve months after my consecration, I served as Bishop Coadjutor, and I had been the diocesan for less than a year when the crisis at Little Rock came to a head.

3

*For these reasons it seemed appropriate, at first, to keep myself from involvement in the crisis. To be sure, I had been reared in Texas, educated for the priesthood in Virginia, and had exercised my ministry only in the South. But I was new to Little Rock and still considered myself somewhat of an outsider. Furthermore, I was to spend the rest of my life here, and if things did not go well, both my own work and that of the Church as a whole might suffer for a number of years. Therefore, the question that constantly posed itself was: Is this issue an important enough one to risk the future on?*

*I have finally decided that it is.*

*There is a spiritual involvement in every issue of this kind which always demands initiative from the Church. The Gospel has something to say to this situation, and the office of a bishop designates him to say it. So much, then, for the decision to play a part in the Little Rock crisis. And it seems equally evident that what experience has taught us here should be offered, in all humility, for the understanding and assistance of others.*

*However, at the outset it should be made clear that there is no intention in this report to pass judgment. It is not designed to single out any individual or individuals for public condemnation. The sole purpose is to explain and, by explaining, to assist in the Church's ever-continuing Ministry of Reconciliation.*

As the world passes from crisis to crisis, the Little Rock story moves from front-page prominence to an obscure place on the inner pages, and back again into the headlines. Wherever the events are chronicled, it has become evident that here is not merely a story of racial conflict, nor one merely of community concern. States' rights, the authority of the Supreme Court, the moral duty of the Christian, the Church's mission—all these elements in the Little Rock "situation" are intertwined with the segregation issue. What is happening here is in part historical and in part contemporary, and its effects are reaching out over the nation and the entire world. For, as John Donne so wisely wrote: "No man is an Island, entire of itself; every man is a piece of the Continent, a part of the main; if a clod be washed away by the sea, Europe is the less . . . any man's death diminishes me, because I am involved in mankind; And therefore never send to know for whom the bell tolled; it tolls for thee."

In this context, the angry cry of a mob in front of Central High School was not the isolated shout of a few deceived people. It was the representative clamor of unthinking man, beginning in a whisper and swelling gradually into a stentorian roar which covered the earth. These many months later it continues to echo and reecho against the mountains of prejudice, pride, and insecurity. Because man is involved in mankind, it is still being heard in the North and the South, in Europe and Asia, in Africa and Australia. And the bells could be tolling right now.

## LITTLE ROCK

Little Rock, affectionately named "The City of Roses," is reported to be one of the friendliest communities in the South. Its people have a way of clasping your hand warmly in both theirs and emphasizing each word of their greeting

5

or farewell. In conversation they reach over to touch your arm affectionately. On the street, when your eyes meet theirs, whether stranger or not, they are quick to respond with an uninhibited "Howdy." As you drive past in your car, they raise one finger from the steering wheel as a sign of greeting to friend and stranger alike. *Time* was correct in describing Little Rock as "a pleasant, leisurely place of well tended homes and green lawns where violets and jonquils bloom in spring, and chrysanthemums in autumn." (*Time*, Oct. 7, 1957)

The city—in a very real sense Arkansas' only city—lies toward the center of the state. Designated as the capital in 1820 and incorporated in 1825, it continued to offer leadership first to the territory, then to the state. Its metropolitan area comprises some 243,000 people. Percentagewise, the Little Rock population is 75% white citizens, 24% non-white, and 1% foreign-born. Although there has been a rapid influx of out-of-state residents since World War II, most of the people are native Arkansans from small communities or farms, who have brought with them their deeply ingrained southern traditions.

Little Rock has also had a tradition of individualism of which the people have always been proud. This showed itself in the last two national elections when, with Pulaski County, it gave President Eisenhower good majorities both times. In recent years the city has even had a Republican mayor.

The industrial growth of the metropolitan area has been slow, steady, and continuing. The growth of community facilities has kept pace with this residential and

6

industrial growth. The metropolitan area has 200 churches, while Little Rock itself has 14 modern hospitals, 3 public high schools, 6 junior high schools, and 24 elementary schools. The Medical College of Arkansas, the University of Little Rock, the Arkansas Law School, as well as 4 liberal arts colleges for Negroes, and a number of other educational institutions, contribute to the high educational standards the community enjoys.

Little Rock has taken special pride in its Central High School, the plant and stadium of which occupy two square blocks close to the center of the city. The high school has enjoyed an excellent national standing; approximately 56% of its graduates go on to college. A consistently large number of National Merit Scholarships are awarded to its seniors. Until September 1957, Central was the only high school for white students in Little Rock, which undoubtedly explains the strong loyalty and pride which both its graduates and the community have had in it.

Little Rock has been successful in establishing better race relations than almost any other southern city of comparable size. Its symphony, opera, and little theatre have afforded cultural entertainment for both races. All public transportation is desegregated. The Negro has worked alongside the white in factories and has sent his qualified children to the same state-supported colleges. Much employment in the city is bi-racial, and although the whites are sometimes too patronizing and the Negroes too nervously insistent, the relations have generally been good. The only slight ruffle to be found is in a shade of tone which the longtime resident uses to explain to the visitor, as he

7

invariably does, that Little Rock endured a lengthy occupation by Federal troops during the "War Between the States."

Little Rock, then, is a community differing little from any other thriving community of like size. Its interests are the same as those of any other southern city, its citizens are not distinguishable by less literacy or religion. Yet this is the city where, on September 23, 1957, a crowd of whites assembled outside Central High School to curse and threaten nine Negro children. No wonder its citizens continue to shake their heads in bewilderment and ask, "Why?"

## THE SUPREME COURT DECISION
## AND LITTLE ROCK

This story had its beginning May 17, 1954, when the United States Supreme Court delivered its now famous decision, ruling racial segregation in the public schools to be unconstitutional. Five days later the School Board of Little Rock announced its intention to comply with this decision as soon as the method for desegregation was outlined and the time allowed for compliance established. During the following August, however, the National Association for the Advancement of Colored People (NAACP) petitioned the School Board for a program of immediate integration.

By the following spring the school officials had devised and adopted a plan for compliance under which the high school grades would be integrated gradually beginning in September, 1957. There was one proviso, namely, that Hall High School be built and occupied by that time. If this

8

were accomplished by then, according to the plan, the remaining classes were to be integrated over a six year period with the lower grades the last to be affected. It was further agreed that students of both races were to be permitted to transfer to the nearest schools where their race was in the majority, providing their race was in the minority in the school where they were presently enrolled. This procedure, it was felt, would offer a minimum integration in the beginning and provide the safest approach to it.

In late May, 1955, the Supreme Court instructed all local school boards to prepare to integrate "with all deliberate speed." In Richmond, Virginia, the *News-Leader* indicated that this phrase means "a long course of lawful resistance" and the paper called for pledges "to litigate this thing for fifty years." In Alabama, former Governor Talmadge of Georgia urged abolition of all public schools and economic boycott of all "scalawags and carpetbaggers." Mississippi offered five candidates for governor, all of them avowed segregationists. But Little Rock proceeded in its efforts to comply with the Supreme Court ruling and interpreted "with all deliberate speed" to mean "as soon as practicable."

On January 24, 1956, twenty-seven Negroes attempted to register at Little Rock schools at all grade levels but were advised that the schools were not yet prepared to receive them. The following month parents and children, at the urging of the persistent NAACP, demanded immediate and complete integration in all schools in Little Rock and charged that thirty-three Negro children had been refused admission solely because of race. School officials contended that this demand for immediate integration

9

was "unwise, unworkable and fraught with danger." In August, 1956, Federal Judge John E. Miller dismissed the NAACP suit, declaring that the School Board was acting in "utmost good faith" in pursuing its plan for gradual integration. However, he also retained jurisdiction in order to rule whether the board progressed satisfactorily with its plan. Unsatisfied, the NAACP appealed.

Meanwhile the Arkansas legislature moved toward the enactment of four "segregation bills," and in February, 1957, the State Senate gave final legislative approval to the creation of a Sovereignty Commission, to the removal of the mandatory school attendance requirement at all integrated schools, to a requirement that certain individuals and organizations register according to their affiliations, and to the authorizing of school boards to use school funds to fight integration, should they so desire. These bills, and particularly the one creating the Sovereignty Commission, were contested by many Arkansan white clergymen on the grounds that they would grant excessive power for witch hunting and prove an unjustifiable means of circumventing the Supreme Court decision. The Governor, however, signed all four bills into law the following week.

In spite of this rising statewide opposition, Little Rock again expressed its moderate attitude the following month. Wayne Upton and Henry V. Rath, two School Board candidates, ran on a moderate platform of gradual integration in accordance with the adopted plan and were elected by a wide margin over their opponents, both of whom were segregationists.

Meanwhile, a series of legal suits and decisions continued. In April the U. S. Circuit Court of Appeals at St.

Louis upheld the School Board's plan of gradual integration and denied the pleas of the NAACP suit of February, 1956. On August 16, 1957, ten Arkansas Negro ministers filed a suit in the Federal District Court, contesting the validity of the four segregation acts passed by the State Legislature. Also in August, Mrs. Eva Wilbern, the mother of a Central High School student, sought an order in the Pulaski Chancery Court which would permit any Central High School student, so wishing, to transfer to a segregated school. Then Mrs. Clyde Thomason, another Central High School mother, sought a temporary injunction against school integration. This suit proved to be the fuse that lighted the eventual explosion.

On August 29, the Pulaski Chancellor, Murray Reede, granted the requested temporary injunction, basing his decision primarily on the testimony of the Governor, who had been called as a witness. Governor Faubus testified that in his opinion integration at this time would lead to violence. The next day Federal District Judge Ronald N. Davies nullified the Pulaski Chancery Court injunction and ordered the School Board to proceed with its plan of gradual integration to start September 3, the opening day of school. He also issued an order that enjoined "all persons in any manner, directly or indirectly," from interfering with the integration plan. But by this time rumors were abroad and tensions markedly increased.

In an editorial (Sept. 1) the *Arkansas Gazette* stated: "We do not believe any organized group of citizens would under any circumstances undertake to do violence to school children of any race." There were other such statements. From this point, however, until September 23, there was

11

almost a daily succession of events that moved in dramatic fashion towards violence.

## CENTRAL HIGH SCHOOL OPENS

On Labor Day evening Governor Faubus ordered the Arkansas National Guard to Central High School. He based this action, first, on "evidence of disorder and threats of violence" and, second, on the fact that litigation on the recently passed integration laws was still in process. In view of the Governor's action the Little Rock School Board, caught now between the ruling of the Supreme Court and the action of the state, requested the nine Negro students who had registered not to attempt to attend school. On the third day, Judge Davies ordered integration to begin the next morning while the Governor announced that the National Guard would remain at Central High School.

The following morning the Negro students made their way to the entrance of Central High School through a cordon of jeering, booing white teenagers, but they were turned back by the guards. A large crowd of adults had also gathered at the urging of the League of Central High School Mothers, the members of which had been on the telephone the night before, inviting parents of the students to gather this particular morning. There was much hooting and hissing by the crowd as the Negroes were leaving.

Up to this point Mayor Woodrow Mann and the police had maintained they could find no basis in fact for a claim of violence, but by this time violence was perceptibly in the air. The School Board, therefore, requested the Federal District Court to suspend temporarily its integration plan. Meanwhile President Eisenhower had advised Governor

Faubus that the Federal Constitution would "be upheld by every legal means" and asked him to give "full cooperation to the United States District Court." In reply, Governor Faubus offered to share his evidence of threatened violence with the Federal authorities. On Saturday Judge Davies denied the School Board's request for a temporary suspension of their plan and ordered Central High School to be integrated the following Monday.

Later, the Justice Department in Washington directed the Federal authorities to bring proceedings for an injunction against the Governor and two National Guard officers to prevent them from interfering with public school integration. On Saturday Governor Faubus conferred with the President at Newport, Rhode Island. Judge Davies ruled on his return that the Governor had not used the troops to preserve law and order and enjoined him and the Arkansas National Guard from interfering with the integration plan. The Governor's attorneys, in an extraordinary move, stated their case and walked out of the hearing. In the early evening the Governor removed the troops from the High School before departing for a meeting of the Southern Governors' conference at Sea Island, Georgia.

### BLACK MONDAY

The climax was reached the following Monday, September 23, when 1,000 white people gathered very early outside the school. They cursed, shoved, tore their hair, and wept when they learned the nine Negro students had been taken through a side entrance. Not many in the crowd had seen the Negroes approach. A diversion had occurred when

13

several in the crowd turned suddenly on some white newspaper men and photographers, knocking one of them down, pushing, shoving, and hitting the others. A police patrol finally broke through to intervene and remove the newsmen. Then, attention was called to the Negro journalists who were approaching. Members of the mob jumped on the back of one of these journalists and wrestled him to the ground. Others mauled and kicked him. He was saved from serious injuries by the cries, "The niggers are in our school," "Let's go get those niggers," and to the white students peering out of the windows, "Come on out. Don't stay in there with those niggers." There was a sizeable group of mostly middle-aged women who shouted and wept as they urged the men on.

Meanwhile, fearful parents having heard of the violence began to arrive at the school to get their children. The mob continued to push at the police barriers, to scream and threaten. From the reports of objective authorities the limited number of local police performed admirably in keeping order at the barriers but were insufficient to patrol the peripheries where the attacks occurred. There was grave concern lest the police themselves would be rushed. One policeman reported later that, in all of his years of experience, he had never seen a mob with the fanatical look this one had. Finally, it was agreed that the Negro students should be removed. That was the end of it. Throughout the day in various parts of the city there were other encounters between the races, though no mob rule or pandemonium. The Police Department was strained almost to the breaking point but was successful in preventing citywide violence.

As social psychologists have noted before, here too, in Little Rock, the mob became man's chief hiding place and his certain escape from individual responsibility. In this crowd, on Black Monday, there was many an individual who committed an act of violence which he would have had neither the courage nor the viciousness to commit alone. What he would not have dared, face to face and by himself, he accomplished without restraint under the incitement of others.

President Eisenhower called this rioting disgraceful and signed a proclamation clearing the way for use of Federal troops to enforce order. The next day 1,100 officers and men of the 101st Airborne Division moved into Little Rock, having been flown here from Fort Campbell, Kentucky. The Arkansas National Guard was also placed under Federal order and mobilized.

But what the average citizen here still wants to know is how all this could ever have happened in Little Rock. This *is* a moderate, normal American city. Its people are law-abiding. It is simply incomprehensible to them, regardless of any personal convictions on integration which they might have, that such infamy should blacken their community. The pall which descended upon the city when the troops moved in is indescribable. Citizens asked themselves, "Can this really be happening to us?"

### SOME ANSWERS TO "WHY" AND "HOW"

The aftermath, accordingly, has been a continued querying of "Why?" and "How?" Was Little Rock chosen by contending forces because of its temperate atmosphere and therefore a good testing ground for all concerned? Is the veneer of civilization so thin that man will even today resort to physical violence and uninhibited emotion when the forces of law and order are lessened or removed? Can a gathering of the merely curious be whipped into the fanatical pitch of a rabble by a small minority of zealots? Does a man automatically commit all manner of evil without reason or compassion or responsibility once he is lost in the anonymity of the crowd?

These are a few of the questions which Little Rockians are attempting to answer these days. And their queries must not be discounted as the self-vindication of a remorseful people. The proper diagnosis of a disease must always precede its cure.

One of the theories advanced today by way of answer contends that the build-up of opposition to integration at Central High School has in no small manner been organized, inspired, and financed from outside Little Rock—and even from outside the state. Although evidence of threatened violence has never been published, there is a persistent rumor to the effect that a thousand cars, filled with armed men, were prepared to ride into Little Rock that Labor Day weekend. Law enforcement officials must have given the rumor some credence, for police cruisers were stationed at several highway intersections leading into the city. The caravan did not materialize, but a number of out-of-city cars did enter the city Tuesday morning. The occupants of these cars had to ask for directions to Central High School, so unfamiliar were they with the community and one of its best known landmarks.

Another factor favoring this theory of "out-of-the-city"

16

support has been the extension of the programs of various organizations. Their increased advertising, their expanded circulation of handbills and mailing pieces, their stepped-up purchase of television and radio time, all bespeak financial backing. It could have come entirely from this community, but the number of speaking tours being undertaken throughout the South by local leaders seems to indicate otherwise.

Such evidence is admittedly circumstantial. Nevertheless, it has led a good many moderate citizens to believe that their city has been specifically selected for a battleground and that local citizens have been spurred on by others who preferred to have the battle lines drawn elsewhere than in their own front yards.

Another recurring query questions the degree to which politics are a factor. In recent state elections extremist candidates had been defeated by the advocates of a moderate platform; and in the election of March, 1957, the two moderate candidates for the School Board were successful over their segregationist rivals. When the proposal to change the city's aldermanic administration to a managerial form of government was put before the electorate in November, 1956, the victory of the managerial form was unquestionably due to the good offices of the group of restrained citizens called the "Good Government Committee." The outcome of all these elections, therefore, indicated a desire for conservatism on the part of the state and the city.

However, the atmosphere began to change. Governor Marvin Griffin of Georgia and ex-State Senator Roy W.

Harris were invited to Little Rock immediately prior to the school opening to address the Capital Citizens Council. Governor Faubus appeared in Chancery Court and testified of his fear of violence. The Capital Citizens Council (C.C.C.), which had been incorporated in 1956, became extremely vocal, and the National Guard was moved to the school to prevent violence. Was this series of events organized by someone behind the scenes with a political motive in mind? Was the integration issue at Central High School deemed a good issue on which to gain popular support? Such questions remain unanswered—but they have not ceased to be asked.

Commerce and industry are also mentioned in this connection. The state has a large industrial development program under way. Heavy Federal support is being added to meet highway needs, the building of dams, and the erection and expansion of military installations. While the eye of suspicion is generally cast in such directions whenever "politics" are mentioned, it is assuredly raised here as the question is asked whether big business is trying to enter politics through the door of the integration issue.

#### THE IMPLICATIONS OF INTEGRATION

Whatever the truth may be, September 23 found the average citizen completely unprepared for violence and disorder. Yet once violence had occurred and the Federal troops were moved in, clear-cut issues began quickly to pyramid upon each other.

First of all, there was the obvious social implication of racial integration. It does no good to discount southern

18

attitudes in this respect or to condemn them as racial prejudice, denial of brotherhood, or unpatriotic revolt against Federal law. The Southerner has a lot to adjust to, but condemnation will not quicken his transformation. His attitude toward the Negro is something that has been deeply ingrained for generations and requires understanding. In a section of the country where numerical superiority quite often lies with the colored, he has built up a real fear of becoming engulfed by a race he regards as inferior to his own. In a region still sensitive to the demands of chivalry, he is not a little concerned about the possible consequences of integration upon his family. Trained and educated himself, he is very uneasy about the future since most of his experience has been with a class of Negro which has not taken advantage of the educational opportunities offered.

The average Southerner rarely has an opportunity to see what a Negro is capable of becoming. And when his racial pride appears to be threatened by an assertive, organized people who have never before had the temerity to make demands, he instinctively moves to protect himself. It is contended occasionally that the present state of things is due to southern unwillingness to grant the Negro dignity and opportunity. This is debatable, but in any case placing the blame does not, at this juncture, make the problem any less real.

Extremists know this full well. They deal in terms like "mongrelization" and "race-mixing." When they began to move, advertisements appeared in the Little Rock newspapers asking such questions as: "Are Negroes and whites to join in the same high school plays and participate in the love scenes together?" "Are Negro girls to use the showers and other facilities our daughters use?" "Are the high school dances to be open to both races without discrimination?" The explosion was immediate throughout the state.

Intelligent Christian people confide that they know it is dreadful to discriminate. They acknowledge that Christ died for *all* men, regardless of race; they agree that integration must come and that it ought to come. Yet they cannot refrain from "a queer feeling inside" whenever they sit by a Negro or see him "at home" in the presence of whites. They recognize this is wrong, but the only solution they know is that of more time—time to adjust themselves and time for the southern Negro to grow in the responsibilities of citizenship.

### THE STATES' RIGHTS ISSUE

The second issue involves the continual States' rights vs. Federal rights controversy. The Supreme Court decree has been under attack by the South from the moment it was handed down. There is honest conviction on the part of legally trained Southerners, and of many Northerners, that aside from the integration ruling, the willingness of the Supreme Court to judge this case is, in the first place, in itself a violation of States' rights. The order for Federal troops to occupy Little Rock is deemed the greatest violation of all.

Senator A. Willis Robertson of Virginia stated in *U.S. News and World Report* (Oct. 18, 1957) that the "use of the army in civil-rights cases is clearly illegal." He defined such an action as an "ill-advised assault on the fundamental principles of the constitution" and "of the rights guaranteed to states by the tenth amendment." Columnist David Lawrence insisted that the President's Proclamation was based upon a reconstruction statute of 1871, the constitutionality of which has never been tested in court. Mr. Alfred J. Scheweppe, formerly Dean of the University of Washington Law School, also maintained in *U.S. News and World Report* (Nov. 1, 1957) that Article 2, section 3, of the Constitution which provides that the President "shall take care that the laws be faithfully executed," refers only to "laws" which are Acts of Congress and not to Federal court decrees. And the *Saturday Evening Post* (Oct. 26, 1957) editorially questioned both the rights and the wisdom of "the Administration's effort to force this policy [of integration] on the South by means of court injunction followed by Federal military action." Such views are quite representative of an area in the United States which has never forgotten that it once fought a war for States' rights and that it was occupied by Federal troops.

The decree of the Supreme Court plus the action of sending troops into Little Rock cannot for a moment be by-passed as inconsequential. When the 101st Airborne Division moved in, there was surprise, dismay, in some instances relief, but in no small measure indignation. A great many people who had previously admitted the right of integration (at least in principle) were instantly repelled by the Federal action. It is even safe to say that more support for integration might have been forthcoming had it not been for the States' rights issue. The foes of integration immediately beclouded peoples' minds and, in many instances, eased their consciences with their arguments for States' rights. The stickers issued by the thousands, pro-

21

claiming the car's occupants to be "Refugees from Oc-cupied Arkansas," have nothing to do with the integration issue at Central High School, but it has become so thoroughly confused with the first issue that today few people are willing or capable of distinguishing between the two.

## VIOLENCE OR LAW AND ORDER?

The final issue, of course, is whether to rule by violence or by law and order. This would scarcely seem an issue in our intelligent, civilized society; yet if what has been actually said, and continues to be said, by the zealous opponents of integration and segregation alike, is carried to its logical end, then there can be no other conclusion but violence.

Mail is continually being sent out by the League of Central High School Mothers and the C.C.C. On the envelope there is a figure of a soldier with a bayonet pointed at two school girls, and around this the words "Remember Little Rock." The question generally asked is: "What can we do to stop integration?" and the meetings held are specifically for the purpose of dealing with this question. One of the meetings had a clergyman speak on the subject, "Shall we quit the fight—what is our hope?" Also there have been flyers sent out on which appeared the photograph of Mrs. Daisy Bates, the head of the local NAACP, showing her with the criminal's number that was hung around her neck when she was brought before the Little Rock Police Department back in 1946. In bold type the flyer begins, " 'Mrs.' Daisy Bates, Little Rock's 'Lady' of the year." Then it continues, "Parents: do you know

22

. . . (1) That there is a vicious fear campaign in process at Central High School, whereby the white children are being told that at any time a white child has trouble with a Negro student that the white students must face Daisy Bates and be cross-examined by her; (2) That an iron-clad censorship has been clamped on Central High School; (3) That Jess Matthews, principal, has imposed an almost prison like fear upon the white students against talking even to their parents about what is going on in Central High School; (4) That Daisy Bates has free access to the school and Jess Matthews' office, and is seen frequently in Matthews' office; (5) That Daisy Bates was allowed to cross-examine a number of white students recently, following a kick fight between a white girl and a Negro girl. Because the white girl would not answer Daisy Bates' questions, Mr. Matthews gave the white girl two weeks in detention hall. Who is running Central High School, [Superintendent of Schools] Blossom or Bates—or both?"

If confronted by the question whether he wanted violence instead of law, there is not a man or woman in Little Rock who would answer "Yes." But the emotions, bordering upon religious fanaticism, which have been manifested and the fierce, irrational accusations which have been heard—all add fuel for the burning.

When one attempts to answer the "Why" of this attitude, he soon must confess his inability to do so. Perhaps it is easier for some people on both sides, by virtue of their limited backgrounds, to take a position and fight behind it, as behind an infallible authority, rather than to come out into the open field of arbitration where mind is

23

pitted against mind. In any case, closed minds and fiery emotions, unless contained, have but one inevitable end— violence.

This is true of both extremists and moderates, segregationists and integrationists. Some readily confess their conformity to law and order and their opposition to mob rule. Then they add, "But we are not going to let anyone force niggers upon us." Such an attitude in the face of possible violence stands as a constant paradox. A well-educated segregationist lady says, "There are many things worse than violence." An integrationist from Warwick, New York, writes, "God, what weak milktoasts you all are." Another segregationist woman writes from Alabama, "I am an Episcopalian, but I will see every one of the black b . . . 's in Hades before I would give one a crust of bread." Such statements are not unrepresentative of the emotions of both North and South, as well as of people in Little Rock. And any claim to law and order is refuted by such vocal opposition. So it is still a moot question whether or not the first two issues involving segregation and States' rights are to be permitted arbitration by reason and legal action.

This, then, is a brief review of the present Little Rock situation. It could change in a variety of ways before these words are published. Looking back over what has occurred, it has to be admitted that there are many southern areas where the school boards could not have proceeded as far as did Little Rock's School Board, where the citizens would have been more vehement in their resistance to integration—indeed, where the Governor would have moved as did the Governor of Arkansas. It would seem to those who know the South, and its attitude towards these problems, that Little Rock, a moderate city in the Southwest, was chosen by design to be the ground for the battle; first, because it offered, in its moderation, the best chance of success according to the thinking of each separate party; and secondly, because what is decided here in this moderate city will be far "bigger than Little Rock."

# 2

# COMMUNICATION
# BREAKDOWN

From the moment of the Supreme Court's ruling, some three years ago, Arkansas has experienced a slow, but progressive, deterioration in normal communications, especially between the white man and the Negro. Self-consciousness has reduced conversation between the races to an embarrassed, formal, artificial thing. Mutual suspicion has become so pronounced that neither race willingly trusts the other. And there is no little fear among both white and black alike as to what the other might be planning in secret through the NAACP or the C.C.C.

26

In a remarkably short period both races have been thrown back upon themselves by this estrangement. Their self-consciousness and fear have built high walls around their minds, and no method has yet been devised by either for breaching these walls and reaching the other. This, in turn, has created an inability and unwillingness to seek any solution to segregation and integration other than their own, and that without reference to the other. Both take the position, "Here I stand, I cannot do otherwise." True, white man and Negro continue to talk about the need for understanding and open-mindedness, but the crux of their plea is always that the other race needs to understand and be open-minded—never their own. While claiming objectivity, actually both have closed their minds.

Humor has its own flavor of truth in this respect. A man from the Arkansas Delta country recently called one of his friends in Little Rock and took the occasion to make absurd accusations concerning one of the leaders in this controversy. His Little Rock friend replied in fairness, "You are all wrong about that man. He is not the sort of person you think, at all. If you will drop by the next time you are in the city, I will convince you." To which the Delta resident replied with a roar, "But that's the trouble. I don't want to be convinced!" and slammed the phone down hard. It is this sort of thing which lends point to a sign that we see these days: "My Mind Is Already Made Up—Don't Confuse Me with the Facts."

To offer yet another illustration: The governing body of a certain congregation was convened by its minister for the purpose of discussing this issue. When it learned the reason for the meeting, its first motion stated that the

27

meeting was not to be recorded in the minutes as having been convened; its second motion was for adjournment. The helpless minister had to throw up his hands in despair. There was no resentment at his effort. His laymen showed a certain affectionate admiration for his having made the effort. Yet their minds were made up, and they did not want to be "confused by the facts."

## BETWEEN WHITE AND NEGRO

In such ways has communication broken down in practically every area of human relationships. Many a planter has said, almost in a spirit of desperation, "I can't talk to my people any more. When I try, they look at the ground, kick the dirt, and answer me in a single word. The younger Negroes scarcely answer at all. A few months ago we had normal conversations about the crops, the church and our families. Now it is only 'Yes, sir' [and 'No, sir'] and I don't know what to do about it."

The concern of these planters for the Negro is real and affectionate. Call their way of life old-world and outmoded, if you will. But it produced, let us not forget, a mutual understanding between the races that in no small way carried over into the southern cities. The white man has watched over "his people," provided medical care, schooling, clothing, even church buildings for their worship. He has looked after them and, in return, has received a ready response. This is not to imply that such a life is to be preferred to greater dignity, better salaries, more comfortable housing conditions, and freedom of initiative for the Negro workers. But at the same time there has been this strong parent-child feeling which is too clearly manifest

28

for anyone to pretend that it does not exist. However, it is this regard of the white individual for the individual Negro that has been destroyed by the breakdown in communication. The former affection has been replaced by self-consciousness, suspicion, fear and, at the last, by red hot anger at the repulse.

It is no different with the Negroes. Those who know them have recognized, particularly among the young, that they are possessed of a new zest, a new vitality, and a new urgency to claim their rights. They have sensed that their day is near at hand, and it is no wonder that they are eager to have it! Yet, at the same time, they, too, are hesitant about breaking the bond which has existed between them and their white people. They would like to find some way to keep it and, at the same time, attain their new life. They realize that their affiliation with the new is a betrayal of the old and that it stands in direct opposition to the white man's wishes. They feel sure that even as they have joined the NAACP, he has affiliated with the C.C.C. So there is the same confusion and the same self-consciousness. Better not inquire. Better not talk about it. Better say only "Yes, sir" and "No, sir."

For the person not born and raised in the South all this may be difficult to understand. There is nothing in the North, or even in the great central prairie regions, to compare to the southern plantation way of life. The light of mutual affection in the eyes of a southern white man or a southern Negro has to be seen to be appreciated. The tragic plight of the southern black man as he tries to clasp a new freedom and dignity with one hand, while endeavoring to hold on to his old anchors with the other, is like

29

that of a child starting to school for the first time, who is eager in his desire to be out in the world, yet looking back over his shoulder every few steps to the security of parent and home. Perhaps the time has come for separation—but the transition has its pain. Apprehension, doubt, fear, zeal that knows no diplomacy, an urgency which pushes ahead, the demand to be heard—all join together to erect barriers which so far have not been breached.

### BETWEEN NEGRO AND NEGRO

Naturally, these same emotions have spread within the races themselves. Negroes have become more and more wary of each other, and so have whites. In Little Rock approximately one-fourth of the colored people are still crying, "We don't want integration. Leave us alone." The remaining three-fourths are insisting, "Give us our rights." Many a Negro says of the NAACP, "They're not our kind of people." He confides that he wishes there were no such organization and that all he wants is to be permitted to mind his own business. However, in nearly every instance the speaker is over forty with a long plantation life behind him. The younger Negroes, on the other hand, are avid for what is their due. Some insist that once given, they do not necessarily mean to take it. They explain, "We do not intend to go to white schools, but we want the *right* to go to them if we choose." This is a common statement, at least in Virginia, Texas, and Arkansas; but the whites cannot always believe it.

Still, communications have broken down between these two sides. Those who do not want to become members of the NAACP, or who are alarmed by the tension in the areas where this organization works, and by the incidence of violence that has occurred, try to arrange their work so as not to be on the streets after dark. Furthermore, they are fearful of what may happen to their children if there is integration. A Gallup poll of December, 1957, predicts that a million and a half of them are seriously thinking of moving out of the South, while a million or more might consider it if trouble should flare up in their immediate area. Some of them even tell the more aggressive members of their race to let them alone. Others join up, but only out of fear of reprisal or to show race loyalty. All these Negroes are apprehensive and have segregated and isolated themselves from the other Negroes.

On the other hand, of the 24,000 colored people in Little Rock, 18,000 are eager for integration. They cannot understand, and consequently are not a little impatient with, those of their race who are content with their lot. They exercise the same suspicion towards them as they do towards the whites. "What are these 'old fashioned' Negroes saying about us?" "Are they spying and informing?" "Better leave them alone, too."

So far there has been no violence within the colored race because of this division, probably for two reasons. The NAACP, though quite intolerant and suspicious of their less aggressive people, do not believe that they possess influence enough to pose a threat. And, again, there is the age and educational difference. The older Negroes who do not want change can offer neither a physical resistance nor a thought-out program of opposition. So an uneasy truce

31

exists between the two; and with the line of communication broken down between them, a deep chasm exists between Negro and Negro.

## BETWEEN WHITE AND WHITE

There was a time when white people could discuss the problems and principles involved in integration without raising their voices. Civic organizations could hold meetings, invite Negro as well as white educators to speak, and hold question periods—all in a calm, serene atmosphere of intelligent discussion and debate. In recent times this has become impossible. There was a day when, with Negro servants in the kitchen, a discussion about integration could make polite dinner conversation without embarrassment to either guest or servant. That day has gone. In the past, members of a family could discuss integration and segregation freely and naturally, without fear of arousing emotion. Now, even that time has passed. Indeed, communication has broken down not only between white and Negro and between Negro and Negro, but also between white and white.

The white man's approach these days is to make no approach at all. Longtime friends have learned that their opinions are being supported with too much heat. Business partners have found in many instances that it is a case of being silent or dissolving the partnership. Families are as divided on the subject as they were in 1860. A son takes one position publicly, his mother another. A wife becomes active with one group, her husband with another. Over and over the statements are made: "We simply do not discuss this at home." "It is not mentioned in the office." And, let it be confessed, this breakdown has extended to the Church as well. Some church members are refraining from church attendance and auxiliary meetings, not only because of what has been said in the past but for fear of what may be said in the future. Several clergymen have found it necessary to announce in advance their sermon topics in order to allay any fears that integration was going to be discussed from the pulpit that Sunday. And, of course, in any large social function no one dares to introduce the subject of integration, for he cannot be sure of the others. It is better to say nothing and do nothing. By such attitudes the lines of communication have been destroyed in polite society, and it will take months before they can be restored to their former state of easy understanding.

However, there are several groups of people who do not fear discussion—in fact they welcome it. The C.C.C., the League of Central High School Mothers, and the NAACP are quite vocal. As organizations, they are neither large in number nor representative of Little Rock as a whole; but they are organized. Moderate citizens have not yet learned how to deal with these organizations. Being unorganized themselves, they cannot create a plan capable of combatting agitator tactics. Without doubt no little fear exists among individual moderates lest their names also be vilified in C.C.C. printed advertisements, or on radio or television. So again, there is silence. As far as is known, the general feeling is that it is impossible to maintain or restore communications between the aggressive citizens of Little Rock and the moderate ones.

The NAACP is more subtle. It has to be in the South. It makes few appeals to the public. No advertisements are purchased in the local press, and rarely do its official pronouncements reach the man in the street. There appears to be pressure from its attorneys upon leaders in the controversy with the result that locally there has been an unwillingness to discuss any aspect of the question but the legal one.

## BETWEEN CITY AND STATE LEADERSHIP

Then, more specifically, there is the unfortunate dispute between the leaders themselves. When Governor Faubus called up the National Guard and turned back the nine Negro students from entering Central High School, the public came awake with a shout. Whatever convictions Little Rock had been suppressing came out without inhibition. The Governor was cheered—the Governor was condemned. The Superintendent was false to southern principles—the Superintendent was a saint and a martyr. And, as is always the case, as soon as criticisms were hurled, defenses were erected. Thus communications again were impaired. Two elected leaders—one political, one educational—were made into symbols by the opposing camps.

During this period invectives and accusations flew back and forth across the city so rapidly that it was impossible either to fix responsibility or to essay truth. The breakdown of communication had become so complete among community and state leadership that it was impossible to arbitrate.

Meanwhile, the segregationist program got under way with its scare campaign of abusive mail and anonymous telephone calls. Those which came to the Superintendent

34

and School Board members contained such malicious threats and insane hate that Mr. Blossom had to move his family to a downtown hotel for their greater protection, while School Board members were forced to install unlisted phones in order to save their wives and children from abuse. White students of the high school who had shown a disposition to accept conditions were called regularly, told that the other students would not tolerate "nigger lovers," and promised that something would happen to them if they persisted. Parents were warned of reprisal, too. Even some state legislators received advice about "a slab at the undertakers." Countless businessmen were intimidated with threats of economic boycott. It is impossible, of course, to estimate the degree to which this campaign of nerves caused intelligent, law-abiding citizens to remain silent, but it assuredly had some effect. What many parents would not have hesitated to do in spite of possible consequences to themselves, they were unwilling to do out of fear for the safety of their children. Even on receiving anonymous threats, they refused to protest, for it was just possible that a supposed friend or neighbor had been responsible.

## THE EFFORTS TOWARDS MEDIATION

So then, communication was disrupted not only between white and Negro, Negro and Negro, and white and white, but also between the city and state leadership. The breakdown was so complete that the primary task became that of getting the various leaders to sit down with one another and discuss the situation. Tragically enough, only one man offered to take the lead in such mediation—Congressman Brooks Hays of Little Rock. From the beginning his efforts to establish harmony have been outstanding. He has taken the initiative to work out solutions to the many-sided problems that no one else seems to have been willing, or disposed, to handle.

At City Hall the Mayor and Aldermen, soon to be replaced by a managerial form of government, could do nothing because of the transition. Having contended that the employment of the National Guard on the grounds of expected violence was based on false evidence, they felt forced to withdraw from further responsibility. And because each of the contending elements had its own following, it soon became obvious that there were few leaders in Little Rock who could be recognized as completely objective and concerned only to iron out difficulties through mediation and arbitration.

Consequently, citizens and authorities alike began looking hopefully to the Church. The Governor, the Mayor, the School Board, readily confessed their need for the Church's objective perspective. Each expressed the hope that the Church "would do something." Up to this time, the Church had been active in the situation principally through the efforts of some of its leaders.

All the while the NAACP had maintained its constant pressure against the School Board. Because it was less vocal, its importuning was less apparent. But with the Supreme Court decision behind it and the good will of northern legislatures and citizens alike, it found itself in an extremely favorable position. The Courts would protect its interests. It had nothing to mediate and, in fact, to agree to mediate would be to risk its cause. Therefore, it stood back from efforts at agreement and kept a watchful eye on the School

Board, responding to every resolution or act which appeared to endanger its position.

## WHAT THE CHURCH TRIED TO DO

Mr. William P. Rock, a staunch Episcopal layman and the head of the Industrial Development Commission, for example, was doing a yeoman's work. Over a period of three weeks he had been intently trying to establish a channel of communication between the Governor's office and the Church's leadership. Working well past midnight most of the time, he sought to get beyond blame-fixing and other inconsequential matters, and into the main problem of how to break down the impasse. His efforts involved offering, with the utmost Christian patience and without faltering, a series of proposals and counter-proposals.

The Governor's chief concern at this point was that the people of Arkansas would understand his decision in calling out the Guard and approve it. He had not yet received support from the C.C.C. or, for that matter, from anyone else. He was, therefore, anxious that "someone come forward and help me."

Congressman Brooks Hays, as we mentioned, was also untiring in his task of mediation. He risked his future as a political figure and boldly involved his church—Mr. Hays is president of the Southern Baptist Convention—by continuing his efforts to find a common foundation upon which a solution could be built. He arranged the meeting between Governor Faubus and President Eisenhower at Newport, Rhode Island, on September 14. That meeting seemed to conclude in a spirit of agreement, although there had not been mutual understanding. Despite his efforts,

37

Congressman Hays had finally to admit that he "felt like a sparrow that flew into a badminton game." What the President had taken as the Governor's assurance of compliance with the Supreme Court decision, the Governor had qualified as being dependent upon what the local situation might be from day to day. And when, after several days, Governor Faubus had not found it possible to support the integration ruling by beginning to withdraw the National Guard troops, Congressman Hays could go no further. Nevertheless, he continued to meet with clergy, with civic clubs, the Chamber of Commerce, and individuals in his effort to break the impasse.

Three of the six members of the School Board are Episcopalians, and the others are Baptist, Methodist and Presbyterian respectively. Each is active in his own church. They are able men, and they met with church leaders separately and together many times. Agreeing that mediation was desperately needed, they made themselves available for consultation and advice throughout. But at the same time they had their own honest disagreements even within the Board, and it soon became manifest that a division existed between themselves, let alone an impasse between the entire Board and other parties involved.

At the same time, through the effort of the Rev. James C. Jackson of St. Philip's Episcopal Mission, consideration was given to the possibility of NAACP leaders sitting in conference with the Governor and the School Board. However, after several exploratory contacts, it was decided that no good purpose could be served at the moment by inviting the Negro leaders in; and it was a moot question whether they would come if invited, for to do so would weaken their own position which was very strong indeed.

The Rev. Dunbar Ogden, president of the Little Rock Ministerial Alliance and pastor of the Central Presbyterian Church of Little Rock, was also an active participant in mediation efforts. As an individual clergyman rather than as president of the Ministerial Alliance, he inaugurated many projects and gave countless hours in his attempt to be of service to all the groups involved.

Nor were the ministers of Little Rock silent during this three year breakdown of communications. From the beginning they worked unceasingly to prepare their people for public school integration and to lead the way. As far back as April 6, 1956, they initiated and joined with a group of white and Negro lay leaders under the name, The Arkansas Citizens for Orderly Compliance, to pass the following resolutions:

"As a group of concerned citizens of Arkansas, we accept the decree of the Supreme Court regarding segregation in the public schools. We believe: That enforced segregation of the races is contrary to Christian principle; that enforced segregation of the races is contrary to democratic principles; that the stability of American democracy depends upon respect for and maintenance of constitutional law, of which the Supreme Court is the ultimate interpreter; that the educational progress, industrial development and prestige as a state depend upon wise handling of problems of integration and minimizing of confusion, tensions, and strife; that attempts at evasion or defiance of the Supreme Court's decree are divisive and futile. We pledge ourselves to the principles of orderly compliance and invite other citizens of Arkansas who share any or all of these beliefs to join with us in this expression."

In February, 1957, three Episcopal clergy, the Very Rev. Charles A. Higgins, the Rev. J. Hodge Alves, and the Rev. William A. Willcox, Jr., joined with other ministers of the city and state to visit the State Legislature in protest against the proposed segregation bills and especially HB322 for the creation of a State Sovereignty Commission. Again they pointed out the danger which such a commission would pose to a democracy, as well as its being a violation of Christian beliefs and ethics.

On the afternoon of September 3, sixteen Little Rock ministers including three Episcopal clergymen, issued still another statement. It was the first public protest of the Governor's act of using the National Guard troops to prevent the nine Negro students from entering Central High School.

"We, the undersigned ministers of Little Rock, strongly protest the action of Governor Faubus in calling out the armed forces of the state to surround Central High School, thereby preventing integration in compliance with the Supreme Court's decision of May 1954, and the order of the Federal Court of August 1957.

"We deplore: (1) The overriding of the authority of the local school administration; (2) the disregard of national law; (3) the abuse of the economy of the local school district; (4) the policing of the great majority of the law-abiding youth of the city; (5) the exciting of racial tension; (6) the reflections cast upon our local law enforcement

40

officers; (7) the distraction of the respect of our citizens, young and old, for proper constitutional authority. If violence should now occur in our city, the [state] government must assume a large share of the blame.

"We appeal to every citizen to unite with us in earnest prayer to God that justice will be brought about and a right example set for every child of our community. We call upon the Federal authorities to take steps that will restore public peace and tranquility."

And a week before the opening of school the clergy wrote as follows:

"On Tuesday, September 3, Little Rock's schools take their first step toward desegregation. All of us pray it will be a step taken smoothly. As ministers, we share a heavy responsibility in maintaining a community of good will and understanding. The current rash of lawsuits on the eve of the opening of schools will increase the confusion among school patrons. This adds to the responsibility of all of us during this period of transition.

"Toward meeting his responsibility our respected fellow minister, Marion Boggs, had a 'heart to heart talk' with his congregation at worship on Sunday morning, July 7. We understand the *Arkansas Gazette* will print excerpts of his remarks on Sunday, September 1, on the editorial page. We send this notice, thinking you may wish to do one or more things with the statement on Sunday, September 1, Labor Day Sunday: (1) Read it yourself promptly; (2) ask members of your congregation to read it; (3) read extracts of it from your pulpit; (4) use it as a starter for a statement or

41

sermon of your own. All of us certainly will think and pray much that we may be used for the good of our community at this time—'Thy Will be done.' "

During the entire three year separation period, the ministers had been attempting, from their pulpits, to awaken and guide their people. Preaching Passion Sunday, 1957, on the text "Thy Will Be Done," the Rev. Mr. Willcox, a native of Louisiana, said: "The very fact of segregation inevitably assumed that the race set apart is inferior to the race which sets apart. As a Southerner, I am fully aware of the social complexities which will ultimately be required in the light of the 1954 Supreme Court decision. But I believe that the Christian people of the South will eventually engage in peaceful and orderly compliance with that decision."

The Rev. Mr. Alves, who comes from Alabama, preaching on "The Spirit of the Good Samaritan," said: "In our beloved Southland today we see many who are maligned, hurt or fearful. We see some who are jeered at and subjected to indignities because they are black. Here is our neighbor. What will we do for him? There are some in our community, as in every community, who strip and beat them. There are more who pass by on the other side. We as Christians must care and act as neighbors . . . the dignity of personality and self respect demand we help our Negro brethren to find a full and right place as citizens of this Christian democracy."

Dean Higgins, a native of West Virginia, said from his pulpit on September 8: "Little Rock has seen the foundation of human dignity destroy the blight of slavery; and,

42

later, the foundation of human right establish the equality of women. We are seeing in our day assault on the last barrier [race], and we may live to see it come crashing down as another stone in the builder's foundation which inevitably must be laid and the City of God established. Christian people have a contribution to make to the foundations of the city of Little Rock. It may be a costly contribution, but we should remember our Lord was not put to death for his Sermon on the Mount but for his challenge to the prejudices of his day."

### YET THE IMPASSE

In such courageous fashion did the Church's ministers attempt to show the way—but it was not enough. The breach in human relations had closed the minds of the people with the result that church leaders were attempting to solve these social problems in a vacuum. The clergy could not unravel the snarl—a snarl that no one else as yet was prepared to unravel. The breakdown of communications was the great barrier in Little Rock's attempt to fathom its dilemma. Sermons and resolutions were incapable of overcoming the suspicion and fear and anger which were the source of the breakdown and, therefore, when it seemed that the Church might play a further part, it was obvious that communications had first to be restored before normal relations could be resumed.

All the groups concerned agreed on this. They felt the time was desperately needed to work out an equitable solution. They wanted the people of Little Rock and of Arkansas to recognize this need for time and the possibility of real

43

solution if time were to be had. They did not want a crisis precipitated. But because they were committed and could not be objective, they also wanted some objective source to play the major role. This, of course, was impossible.

Thus, if anything, the efforts at mediation widened the breach rather than closed it. At a time when every concerned person might have been working with others, each was standing still and waiting for someone else to make the initial approach. And when, on September 20, Judge Davies handed down his injunction against the Governor and the two National Guard officers for interference in the normal procedures of integration and the guard was thereby removed from Central High School, there was then no further opportunity for negotiation or mediation or anything else.

In conclusion, it must be admitted that by September 23, the white people of Little Rock had become divided into a number of splinter groups and, because of this division, fell easy prey to small, but aggressive and organized, minorities. The citizens were not able to rise above divisive elements in the integration-segregation issue, in the question of Federal rights and State rights. There was no strength anywhere, no voice speaking with an authority the people would heed. The ministers did their best. They spoke out courageously, worked heroically, but their voices were not heard and their work went unrewarded. Then, when it became necessary to labor for mediation behind the scenes and church leaders volunteered, their emissaries were received with respect but not with that attention that is given to political power or physical might. One recalls how in World War II, when the Pope of Rome issued a statement on strategy, Stalin replied, "How many divisions has he?" In a similar way it was so in Little Rock. Then on violent Monday came the cry, "Let's go get those niggers."

# 3

## HINDSIGHT

That the victory is won is enough for the average participant in a contest to know. Normally, he does not take the
time to examine the reasons for victory or to list the means
by which it was obtained. To lose, however, is to ask
"Why?", to point the finger of blame, wherever possible,
in order to correct any failures and weaknesses, and thus
assure victory in the future. Of course, it is far easier to
look back scornfully to errors that are now obvious than
it is to make right decisions down in the arena when the
issue is being hotly contested. And just as a football coach

46

will several times run off the film of last week's game in order for his players to see, and benefit from, their errors, so the situation that developed in Little Rock must be reviewed again and again if those who are yet to face such a situation are to be helped. Therefore, this chapter is designed to search out error and examine weaknesses—with genuine apology, however, for what will surely appear to be caustic judgment and that superior assurance that always accompanies hindsight.

## LOOKING BACK AT THE
## LITTLE ROCK PLAN

The desegregation plan of the Little Rock School Board can serve as our first subject for review. The initiative in promoting it was assigned to Mr. Virgil Blossom, the Superintendent of Schools. Yet, in spite of the fact that it was three years in the making and promoting, and that he delivered over 300 speeches explaining it, hindsight shows a number of elements in the projecting of it that should be studied. Mr. Blossom is a trained educator, who from the beginning has been sincerely concerned with carrying out the Supreme Court decision on public school desegregation. He has worked energetically, sacrificially and in good faith. Therefore, it must be left to specialists in the field of education to decide whether the School Board's Plan and his promotion of it were adequate. Our task is simply to examine the procedures and compare them with the programs of school boards in other communities.

First, in contrast to the approach of Mr. Omer Carmichael, Superintendent of Schools in Louisville, Kentucky, very little work was done in Little Rock to establish

47

a favorable climate in which integration might take place. The many speeches and addresses that were made in Little Rock were made by way of explanation, not preparation. They assumed the plan to be a *fait accompli* and instructed audiences how the mechanics of the plan would work, never attempting to visualize for them its actual operation in the real world of people. The statistic of white and Negro students was always given. The physical reasons why the elementary and junior high schools were not adequate were recited. The estimate of how many Negro children would actually remain at Central High School under the permissive transfer plan was explained. And always there was expressed the certainty that this was the *only* plan which could be put into operation without difficulty. Nowhere was anything heard about its possible effects upon parents, or children, the NAACP, or segregationists.

In answer, the School Board would explain that up to the last moment there was no reason for feeling that the plan would not be accepted. The recent School Board elections had indicated the community's desire for moderation. The C.C.C. had not been heard from to any degree throughout these three years. State leaders were advised of the plan and there had been no objection from them. "Why" asks the School Board, "was there any reason to anticipate trouble?"

In the second place, a review of this preparation seems to show in part, as one newsman put it, that Mr. Blossom "talked chiefly to himself." That is, he spoke to a limited group on his own economic, cultural, and educational level. The Rotary Club heard him gladly. So did the Lions Club, the Kiwanis Club, church groups, and the Chamber

48

of Commerce. Both the Junior League and virtually every P.T.A. group were spoken to. But other levels of city life were not really reached; hence, there was no opportunity to determine what their resistance or opposition might be. Even in the service clubs, churches, and community organizations there were many who disagreed strongly, but they remained politely silent during these preliminaries.

When Louisville, Kentucky, ended compulsory segregation in its public schools, the integration plan included a "free choice" proposal. Fifty thousand cards explaining the method of integration were mailed to the parents of school children, and the opportunity was given them to choose in order of preference three schools for their child if they so desired—these preferences to be honored, providing they did not overload the capacity of the individual school in question. In addition to giving information officially to concerned parents, the chief merit of this procedure lay in the privilege it granted them of choosing the school they wished for their children. It is interesting that 89 per cent of the parents accepted the schools their children were already attending, and only 11 per cent requested transfers. Psychologically, the procedure had this effect: Once parents made their choice of school, they became affirmatively committed to the proposal for integration.

The Little Rock school officials, on the other hand, felt that their plan was so well accepted that it was unnecessary to call on other community resources for assistance or cooperation. In San Antonio, Texas, the Ministerial Alliance, the civic clubs, and many other agencies were all welcomed and encouraged to play a part in creating the proper atmosphere for school integration. They were offered the

49

special assignment of arranging study groups, were asked to participate in public discussions in the areas where their leadership and influence were important. In St. Louis, Missouri, Dr. Philip J. Hickey, Superintendent of Schools, also asked cooperation of ministers, policemen, teachers, young people, and even captains of athletic teams in preparing the people of that city. Louisville, Kentucky, organized community panels; various Parent Teachers Association units held meetings at which members of the School Board, the administration and supervisory staffs, as well as teachers, principals, clergymen, and civic leaders, were speakers. In some Louisville schools books about Negro children, and the Negro people generally, were put in the libraries so that the white children could begin to understand and appreciate the Negro race. It also experimented with desegregation in an integrated summer school session. Agreement with the Supreme Court decision in these communities certainly was no greater than it was in Little Rock. But, as Mrs. Herbert Zimmerman, president of the Louisville P.T.A. Council, said, the agreed task was "to work for harmony among parents toward desegregation."

In Little Rock, however, such procedures were considered as likely to "muddy the waters." The school officials worked on the principle that the less said the better. The Louisville school system was desegregating completely, whereas Little Rock's plan called only for progressive desegregation. San Antonio had a multiple racial problem that involved Mexicans as well as Negroes. While St. Louis was so much larger, population-wise, it was in a different category. Therefore, the approaches of these committees with respect to local resources were considered not pertinent to Little Rock.

The philosophy "let's not court trouble" carried the day. No faculty meetings were held at Central High School, and no meetings to prepare the students. It seems that even now, months later, instead of the customary monthly faculty meeting at Central High School, there has been only one faculty meeting in four months; and in the same period only one P.T.A. meeting. At each of these meetings every effort was made by the administration to keep the problem of desegregation from reaching open discussion.

Neither was it deemed necessary to define, discuss, or study the possible consequences of desegregation before the opening of school, and the teachers were not encouraged to make their suggestions for improving the plan. Again, in contrast, Mr. Carmichael of Louisville, asked the various principals to hold regular faculty meetings the first semester in order that the teachers might discover and state any problems which should be considered. In this way teachers first examined their own attitudes, and then helped the students with theirs. Central High School teachers were not unanimous for integration by any means. There was real opposition for both social and academic reasons. But the authorities felt that the loyalties of the teachers would override other considerations.

The students apparently have also had only one kind of approach made to them—and that a negative one. "Don't do anything or say anything which will bring discredit on Central High School." There were no attempts during the three years previous to educate them about the principle of

51

integration, or to assign them responsibility on their own level; no willingness to accept their offers of help—and apparently there still is not. More, however, will be said about this in a later chapter.

Brief mention might also be made about disciplinary procedures. No rebellious student has been punished in an effective manner since the school's integration. Seventy-two students, at the instigation of adults, walked out of their classes shortly after the integration began, for which they received a three-day suspension. Inside the buildings there have been incidents of sufficient magnitude to make the administrative staff apprehensive. On several occasions white students have followed Negro students in the halls, yelling insulting remarks. These students have maintained they are within their legal rights to do this and have declared their intention to "make things as miserable as possible for them [the Negroes]." Yet in none of these cases of kicking or cuffing have the aggressors received a strong disciplinary sentence. One white student was expelled and later reinstated on her promise to obey regulations. But for the most part, the school officials appeared to be proceeding on the basis that it is better to keep problem students in school and subject them to the influences of culture and education rather than to expel them. The facts, however, seem to indicate that these students are disciplined just enough to give them the right to cry "martyr," but not enough to enforce their reform. Handmade weapons have been confiscated. Whether they were manufactured out of a teen-age spirit of adventure or with a deadly purpose is not known. Still, in this case too, the discipline has been

52

light and almost hesitant—so much so that some of the troublemakers have become quite bold in their revolt against the presence of the nine Negro students.

In fairness and justification it must be stated that the enforcement of discipline has not been easy. When the Principal suspended a white boy for striking a Negro girl on a Saturday, by the following Monday harassing phone calls from citizens—some his friends—and uncomplimentary anonymous letters had almost deluged him. Another member of the administrative staff received abusive letters from all over the nation when he was reported to have asked guards to search the students in that one of them was suspected of having heavy rubber bands and paper clips. This sort of thing makes the enforcement of discipline very difficult and causes those in authority to hesitate.

And again, at least two of the Negro students have not been helpful in establishing harmony in the buildings. Difficult as it has been, seven of them have maintained dignity and silence, and gained credit for themselves. The other two, however, have been irritants, sticking out their tongues at white students and seeking out incidents that they could report to the Principal's office. One of them has finally been suspended for hurling her food at some white students, although with provocation.

In further justice to the School Board it must not be forgotten that its plan for desegregation was the first *bona fide* one for *gradual* desegregation. Nashville's plan came shortly after, but it was the Little Rock plan which was hailed as a guide-post in the South when it was approved by Judge Miller. In fact, the previous trend in Federal

53

Court decisions had been for immediate and total desegregation. As a gradual desegregation program, it was different from the other plans then in existence.

In this hindsight summary of the school administration, it has to be said that they mistakenly believed their plan would be generally accepted, that they asked for no powerful voices to speak in their behalf, sought no cooperation from other sources, and attempted to meet an abnormal condition as though it were a completely normal and natural one. Whether, in view of later events, any of these possible courses of action would have proved capable of protecting against the crisis is debatable. Nevertheless, it has become evident that desegregation cannot be treated as a simple school problem. It is a city, regional, and national one. The greatest error in judgment seems to be that they tried to treat desegregation as a simple school problem rather than as city, regional, and national.

## HOW THE CITY ADMINISTRATION AND THE POLICE PREPARED

In hindsight we find another series of disappointments when we review the actions taken by City Hall. One of the weakest elements in the entire program for desegregation lies in the fact that the Mayor and Aldermen did not create an official Committee on Human Relations. Had it been organized, such a committee might have played an important and valuable role in what was to follow. As it was, no one was designated to sample public opinion and advise community leadership about the mind and temper of the man in the street. No official group existed which could, by reason of a comprehensive study, formulate for the Mayor and Aldermen a statement that could be adopted as the official position of City Hall. There was no board or committee with the formal authority to advise, educate, or assist other city leaders in preparing comprehensively for desegregation. In fact, up to the time of the actual violence, Little Rock authorities took no position and published no statement of policy.

The city administration, therefore, left the School Board to work out its own salvation. As it has been pointed out, the School Board was content with this, but a backward glance shows that if there had even been someone to collect and weigh the contents of the "Letters to the Editor" columns in the newspapers, a more correct diagnosis of Little Rock's climate might have been made.

There is, to be sure, an unofficial Arkansas Council of Human Relations, which describes itself as "non-denominational, non-political, educational, and bi-racial." Tucked away in a gloomy little office, it has been forced to limit itself to private conferences and the distribution of pamphlets. Although its goal is "to attain through research and action the ideals and practices of equal opportunity for all people," lack of funds has circumscribed its activity; and its very want of official status has aroused the suspicions of those who might have learned something from it. Yet, confined in scope though it was, this Council had the facts. It possessed mountains of information, both sociological and socio-psychological, concerning desegregation and some of its pitfalls. However, as far as is known, it was not called upon to play any part in the integration program.

55

Had it been, city officials might have learned from the report in the *Journal of Social Issues*[1] that successful programs of desegregation depended upon:

(1) A clear and unequivocal statement of policy by leaders with prestige. (2) Firm enforcement of the changed policy by authorities and persistence in the execution of this policy in the face of initial resistance. (3) A willingness to deal with violations, attempted violations, and incitements to violations by resort to the law and strong enforcement actions. (4) A refusal of the authorities to resort to, engage in, or tolerate subterfuge, gerrymandering or other devices for evading the principles and facts of desegregation. (5) An appeal to the individuals concerned in terms of their religious principles of brotherhood and their acceptance of the American tradition of fair play and equal justice.

On these five counts, official Little Rock might be said to have batted an absolute zero. There was no statement of policy, no promise of strict enforcement, no published intention to prosecute violations, no appeal to any group on religious or patriotic principles. And the official silence itself was interpreted by many as evasiveness and subterfuge. Had any of these approaches been put into practice in the summer of 1957, the Little Rock story could have been an entirely different one.

Furthermore, the local police seemed not to have considered the possibility of situations arising out of hatred and prejudice. There were many conferences with Mr.

---

[1] Volume 9, No. 4 (1953), an article by Kenneth B. Clarke entitled "Desegregation: An Appraisal of the Evidence."

Blossom, but no great preparation was made. Again, in contrast, the Southern Police Institute at the University of Louisville held interracial seminars. There was a close coordination between the School Board, Superintendent's office, the Chief of Police, and the county police. Long before the opening of school these organizations had secretly completed their trouble-prevention plans. The danger spots in the community had been marked out, with special officers assigned them, and unmarked squad cars with picked personnel were given specific cruising areas in both the city and the county. Plain clothes officers mingled with known trouble makers, listened for information of what might be coming, and shadowed those who were heard to threaten violence. By this procedure it was known in advance that the Citizens Council planned to picket the schools on opening day and all arrangements were made to meet it.

In Little Rock, after responsibility was thrust upon them by the Governor's withdrawal of the Guard, the local police did excellent work. At no little risk to themselves, they held back a thousand people from entering the high school, protected the Negro children from harm, and rescued victims from permanent injury. From the manner of their performance there seems little doubt that they could have handled the matter from the beginning had they been readied and assigned to do so.

City Hall was also willing to consider the matter as a school problem rather than a community one and approached September 23 with no position, no plan to enforce it and no power. Again, like the School Board, it did not anticipate trouble. Up to the week before the opening

57

of school there had been no outward evidence to support a belief that there would be violence. There were no "incidents," no notable degree of vocal opposition, and no threat of mob organization. However, the trouble did come.

## PRIVATE GROUPS IMMOBILIZED

Individual groups in the community attempted to make some indirect preparation for the introduction of the program. The Ministerial Alliance, because it is an integrated organization, was perhaps the best informed of these. In the atmosphere of its Christian environment there was free and uninhibited discussion of the problems, and mutual understanding of them was achieved. Its members recognized, in a way impossible for non-integrated groups to understand, the need to prepare. The Council of Church Women, also bi-racial in membership, did what it could to promote understanding, as did the officials of the non-segregated public library. The Urban League, although under suspicion, was particularly well informed on the situation as a result of its having brought Negro and white leaders together for discussion. And the bi-racial summer work camps conducted (1957) for teenagers under church auspices had a modicum of success in helping to prepare. Two of the Negro pupils at Central High School participated in that program. However, none of these organizations was sought out, and none proved strong enough by itself either to withstand the attacks of extremists or to make itself heeded by those leaders who were convinced that the best program was no program.

Thus when violence came and community mobilization

was a must, there was still no foundation upon which moderate Little Rock citizens could build. This was one reason for the tardiness of community leaders in coming forward. But there were others. It takes time for a democracy to organize. While a totalitarian system can mobilize quickly on the order of its dictators, a free people can not. Little Rock had first to recover from the shock of violence; then to think through and discuss plans and reach decisions on its own initiative rather than obey some commands from on high. Little leadership was offered even here. There was no central figure in public life around whom moderate citizens could rally, and the means offered by which these moderate citizens could express their own views were severely limited. Added to this was the confusion of issues which made proper discussion more difficult. A great many of those opposing segregation deny the right of the Supreme Court to rule on integration and condemn the President's decision ordering Federal troops into Little Rock. Further, those who disapproved violence and mob rule and were unmistakably for law and order found—because their sympathies were with the reasons, if not the actions, of the extremists—that it took them longer to put first things first and, in fact, to see that what the extremists were doing demanded first consideration. Even at this late writing the moderates have still not organized themselves into any considerable resistance group. They are on the defensive, answering with hesitant rebuttal the strong contentions of the extremists. They have yet to come forward with an affirmative program that can challenge the dominating influence of the C.C.C. or the League of Central High School Mothers, on the one hand, or the NAACP, on the other.

All this, it must be admitted, is disappointing—and frightening—to one who remembers the resignation with which the intelligent, moderate citizens of Germany accepted the aggressive emotional rule of Adolf Hitler.

## THE BREAKDOWN OF
## THE MASS MEDIA

Hindsight further shows that the radio, press, and television were of little assistance in the situation. Mr. Harry Ashmore and the *Arkansas Gazette* have received Pulitzer prizes for their courage and forthright reporting, but even so have been unsuccessful in martialing community leadership. The *Arkansas Democrat* has become the rallying point of the extremists merely because it has tried to walk the middle road. And this situation has kept the issues confused and readers perplexed. Both newspapers are suspect by Little Rockians. One of them has become the target of extremist accusation with the result that many judge it to be a pro-integration paper for "blue stocking" readers with a disdainful indifference to the common man. The other is suspect on economic grounds. It has been accused of throwing straws to the wind before taking any stand, and then, on the basis of public reaction, of acting accordingly. Neither paper has been unwilling to print letters-to-the-editor over fictitious signatures. These letter columns are filled with scurrilous attacks, inflammatory statements, and rabble-rousing suggestions of individuals who are granted the protection of anonymity. Although the Press explains that the original letters are signed, the signers' names are not made public.

The local television and radio stations do not offer in

their programs objectivity, either. The various stations, like the press, take different stands, and from the beginning it has been difficult to get from them unbiased news reports. Time has been purchased for some of the most remarkable presentations—presentations that have been made with a minimum of editing or censorship. The citizens have, therefore, taken the same attitudes toward these media as toward the press. They either support the stations which reflect their point of view, or else suspect them all. This contradiction existing among the various public information services might be defended as a manifestation of the democratic way, but in view of the circumstances one is inclined to recall the famous caution that freedom and democracy do not grant the right to cry "Fire!" in a crowded theatre.

A meeting of these services with responsible community leaders could have done much to establish a healthy atmosphere in the community. There were few, if any, radio or television programs designed to prepare for desegregation. There was no uniform emphasis placed on the need for law and order, no general condemnation of violence, and no common agreement on an unbiased presentation of news. In this connection it is fair to say that the citizens of Little Rock feel the last criticism can be directed against the national press as well. They believe that in this crisis there was a great deal of slanted writing that served no good purpose, and they resent the disservice which this did to their community. At any rate, there was an absence of any working relationship with press, radio, or television.

Some businessmen did come forward. The twenty-five past presidents of the Little Rock Chamber of Commerce convened after the outbreak of violence to condemn the action of September 23, and to seek some solution to the deadlock presently existing in the community. However, disagreement among themselves made their efforts futile. Many admitted publicly that they did not mind saying they were for law and order, but that they were still going to stop integration in Little Rock if they could. This automatically put them off from the others and made their leadership impossible. A smaller group from this committee was asked to meet with the Governor and to prepare a report to the community. By the end of December more than seven revisions of this report were made; still there was no agreement, and the project was about to be scrapped as a failure. Had these businessmen succeeded in agreeing among themselves, it is still doubtful that their findings would have been generally accepted, for it was known that some of them had partisan political and economic connections with other sections of the state.

All this while, the clergy of Little Rock continued their attempt to break out of the strait jacket in which society had placed them. Few of them could have prophesied violence. However, none of them would have cared to deny the possibility of violence, and all of them were apprehensive. Their work with their own congregations put them close to the sentiments of the community. Their meetings in a bi-racial group informed them of the thinking of the Negroes. And the disagreements in the thinking of their fellow clergymen, even in a Christian body, pointed up for them all the many facets this problem had. They knew, therefore, that desegregation could not be a simple procedure. They spoke from their pulpits; offered their services to the School Board, City Hall, and the Governor;

passed resolutions and conducted a few limited programs designed to create a more conducive atmosphere; but throughout the days leading to the opening of school the best they could do was hope that the desegregation program would meet with no mishap. As late as November 27, a group of them talked with the Superintendent of Schools concerning improvement of bi-racial relationships at Central High School, but even then they were told that there was nothing that need be done by them at that particular point.

## UNANTICIPATED POLITICAL IMPLICATIONS

Finally, there were the political implications of the integration program. One of the most politically influential areas of Arkansas lies in the Mississippi Delta country. This is a strong agricultural section of the state where at least three-fourths of the tremendous cotton crop is harvested. Cotton plantations of three to five thousand acres are not uncommon. There is naturally a great deal of wealth in an area providing a state's chief economy. But this is also the area of the greatest Negro concentration and, consequently, of greatest concern over any desegregation plan.

It might have been anticipated that eastern Arkansas would not remain indifferent to any proposals to be carried out in Little Rock. But no effort was made to enlist the understanding of this important constituency of the state. Had legislators from the Mississippi Delta and the leaders from Helena, Forrest City, Marianna, and some of the other communities been invited to discuss these issues

63

from Little Rock's standpoint and given the opportunity to hear the Little Rock Plan, there might have been a different atmosphere: if no happy agreement, at least no opposition.

There was also a disappointing silence from representatives in the state and nation. This was not the case when a Citizens Council spokesman approached Kentucky's Commonwealth Attorney, A. Scott Hamilton, concerning a proposal to picket the Louisville schools. He was told, emphatically, that this could create "a clear and present danger," in which case the pickets would most assuredly be arrested. There were no pickets at Louisville schools. In Frankfurt, Governor Lawrence W. Wetherby, other state officials, and representatives in Congress—all accepted the Supreme Court's decision as binding. Said Governor Wetherby, "Kentucky will do whatever is necessary to comply with the law." Senator Earl E. Clements stated that "Kentucky and Kentuckians have always respected our highest court, and I anticipate orderly steps will be taken to do so in the instant case." Senator John S. Cooper defined the rulings as "a logical result of the Constitution" and felt certain that in spite of difficulties "with good sense and judgment they can be worked out." Not all the congressmen were pleased with the Court's decision by any means, but they all agreed in effect that "the Court had decided and the state will obey."

But very few statements of any sort came from any elected representatives of the people of Arkansas during the explosive weeks of September and October. What statements there have been are concerned chiefly with the use of Federal troops.

To summarize, there seem to have been three major reasons why peaceful desegregation in Little Rock failed. First, the belief that the desegregation issue was only a local school problem and the conviction that the program could be carried out by the school administration without outside aid of any kind played no small part in creating the general state of unpreparedness when school opened, and the indecisiveness with which order was enforced subsequently. Second, the lack of official leadership which left the ship captainless upon an exceedingly stormy sea. There were no experienced public servants to set a course for that large majority of moderate opinion or to speak with authority to the agitated minorities. Third, the failure within the community itself to understand what kind of unity the situation called for. On the one hand, the very calls to unity were mistakenly believed to demand identity of opinion; and on the other hand, each refusal to accept was interpreted as a considered preference for anarchy. That fine razor-edge line at which two opinions can meet and establish common bonds was never discovered. Indeed, suspicion, fear, and pride still obscure it. Meantime, it was more dramatic to be against something than for something. Accordingly, these three instances readied the atmosphere in Little Rock for bewilderment and hate.

# 4

# THE CHURCHES
# DIVIDED

Any failure of society to live up to Christian principle must weigh upon the conscience of the Church. And every failure of an individual church member to manifest the discipline of his Lord necessarily pricks the heart of the pastor who has taken an ordination vow to "teach the people . . . with all diligence." Not that the final responsibility belongs to the Church and its clergy for the failures of mankind—Jesus himself was unable to perform any mighty works at Nazareth. Yet when Church and society fail, the conscientious clergyman cannot but feel that he is somehow to blame, nor can he refrain from the self-flagellating cry, *mea culpa.*

Part of this self-blame arises out of the admitted difficulty ministers have in establishing a unity among themselves. A case in point is the recent meeting of only four clergymen to begin work on a "Little Rock Manifesto" on the desegregation problem. Of the four, one was a legalist, one a perfectionist, one a neo-orthodox theologian, and one a biblical theologian. They worked for hours in an attempt to find some common basis upon which to begin a document which would be assured of acceptance by the other ministers of the community—but without success. They admit now that there will have to be a long series of such meetings before even the preface can be drawn.

Clergymen, like men of other professions, act consistently with their training. What they have learned from their seminaries and the interpretations of their church bodies forms a corpus of truth, and establishes a set of Christian principles, to which their consciences confine them. They want to be open-minded, they strive to admit other points of view. Yet there is always that mental protest, that feeling of disloyalty, and even of smug patronage, when they join with clergy of other persuasions. This is not unnatural; it is the very nature of things. However, it sets up a series of irritating stumbling blocks for them whenever they strive to present a united front to the society they desire to lead.

## DIFFERENCES OF ETHICAL INTERPRETATION

One of the best illustrations of this among the Little Rock clergy, at the time of the community's crisis, grew out of their interpretation of Christian ethics. A solid number were dedicated to the principle of perfection. They permitted themselves to see no grays. The sides of every issue were either of the darkest black or the purest white; and it was exceedingly difficult for them to think in terms of "both-and," for all they could visualize was an "either-or." Consequently, when the problem of integration vs. segregation confronted them, they came out, as could be expected, courageously and fervently for the former. They could see no possibility of compromise on such virtues as brotherhood, personal dignity, the rights of free man, or on such vices as discrimination. Their stand always pointed to the ultimate goal of perfection.

For this they were honored by a second group of clergy, who recognized that the perfect goal must be held high but, at the same time, could only shake their heads sadly as though to say, "God be with you. We can't be with you, but we are all for you." This group might be described as the adherents of a system of compromise ethics. Willingly admitting the rightness of the perfectionist position, they felt equally sure that time, patience, and wisdom were required in order to obtain it and that it was better to compromise on perfection in order to establish a *present* condition which might more nearly approximate it. To them the desegregation issue called for the wisdom of the serpent and the gentleness of the dove. In order to create a part of what Christianity required, it seemed to them better to give a little and to take a little in the hope that the last state of society would be better than the first.

Then, there was a third group that was separated from the other two by the issues themselves rather than by the approaches to them. Their individualistic approach might be one of perfectionism or one of compromise, but they reserved the right to participate or not according to their interpretations of the separate issues involved. Some of them were segregationists, but they could not condone violence. Others were integrationists who would not approve the use of Federal troops. Still others were isolationists who felt the Church and the world were too far apart to ever effect a union. Therefore, they could only give a fractional cooperation, and in some instances no cooperation at all. They were members of the Ministerial Alliance and yet apart from it. On some points they were fervent advocates, on others merely silent listeners; and their fellows could never be sure where they would stand or how they would vote.

### OTHER DIFFERENCES

Another divisive factor resulted from a group of fundamentalist clergymen who for the most part had remained outside of the Ministerial Alliance. Their emphasis was mostly upon the Old Testament, and their procedure that of quoting proof-texts favoring segregation. One of the favorite arguments was that God made the Caucasians white and the Negroes black. Therefore, integration is a violation of God's laws. Another rested on the story of Noah, Ham, and Canaan, and the disobedience of Ham which caused the curse of Canaan and his designation as a "servant of servants." Still another argument based on the Book of Acts was that God, in determining the times appointed and the boundaries of men's habitations, had also shown a divine and separate purpose for each race. And another was that God has even separated the seeds in the field so that the tares are not permitted to grow up with the good seeds. The other clergy, though they could not accept such interpretations of Holy Scripture or their application to segregation, were still anxious to honor these fundamentalist clergymen for their convictions and give them place within the Ministerial Alliance, in the hope of establishing some common bond. However, the fundamentalist preferred to keep apart.

Added to these divisive elements was the additional fact that clergymen are no different from other people in their human frailties. Accordingly, timidity was sometimes apparent, for who could help but estimate the effect his stand might have upon his congregation or question what it could mean as far as his security and the security of his family were concerned. A philosophy of expediency—which must be differentiated from the more sincere compromise ethic—was also seen occasionally. And again, there was the nagging question: Who wants to stir up trouble unless it is absolutely necessary? why do anything when it is possible that "things will eventually work out"? Then there were the hopeless ones who were certain that nothing could be done to lead the agitators along a more peaceful path or to a better control of their emotions.

Perhaps a great weakness of the clergy lay in their naïveté. Trained to think the best of others and to trust in the best, they were continually misled into believing what they were told. On a number of occasions they went before authorities to protest an action or to suggest one, and in almost every instance the assurances and promises they received were accepted without question, but refuted by time. Yet it was exceedingly difficult for them to believe that they were consciously being misled or indifferently answered.

And, of course, the normal day-by-day duties of the clergy were too demanding to permit adequate time for thorough discussion of the many facets of the problem. It was a physical impossibility for many of them to meet frequently. Much that was done had to be done by small committees which were not always representative and which were often forced to make plans or devise programs in a matter of minutes, when hours were needed for the task. Even such committee meetings could not be fully attended. Then, when these committee proposals were brought before the Ministerial Alliance for final action, the larger body could not in one luncheon meeting give them the necessary thought before taking action. So this haste, and sometimes open impatience, had its effect not only in precipitous action, but also upon the members themselves.

Accordingly, when these differences that existed among the clergy combined with the frailties which are the human lot of all men, there is little wonder that the leadership was sometimes lustreless. The impressions received at these meetings was that they truly and sincerely wanted unity, but that their training and their personal choices were an almost prohibitive hindrance to it. In love and affection, the clergy of Little Rock had to confess the existence of disagreements which made a united, effective leadership extremely difficult, and it was for these failures that they were moved, individually and as a body, to repent. There was a general understanding of what this lack of unity would do to an already confused community and also what

71

its continuing effect would be on the ministers themselves. The cry of distress, therefore, was very real, and the prayer for guidance fervent.

## THE UNITY FOUND IN CRISIS

Yet when the violence came, discord among the clergy in the Ministerial Alliance disappeared. There was no longer any loyal adherence to particular points of view or personal pledges to specific approaches to Christian ethics. Each saw that there was work to be done and a stand to be taken. They could not follow what seemed to be expediency, but only what was right, and they did so without thought of the possible consequences to their own futures or to their work among the members of their congregations who disagreed with them.

At the meeting called for eleven o'clock on the morning of September 23, when the crowd was gathered outside Central High School, the prevailing opinion was that, in view of the violence, to remain silent was to condone the sin, and to appear neutral was to commit a real Christian heresy. Whatever theological or biblical disagreements there may have been in the past, there was no disagreement on this. To fail to make a judgment upon such violence was to give consent to its tyranny. To remain inactive in the face of such misguided action as was occurring at the High School was, in effect, to approve it. Therefore, their first action was to send representatives to the Chief of Police asking, in the name of the Alliance, that the crowd be dispersed. This was followed by a protest against violence and a call for order. There was no little sense of outrage manifested at this meeting, and the action taken

72

rang the prophetic change "thus saith the Lord." The police, though polite, were occupied, and the ears of the community were so tuned to the cries of the mob that few heard the judgment.

## THE SCRIPTURAL MANDATE

The clergy anticipated this, and while knowing they might not be heard, they knew they had to speak. Behind their words lay first the conviction that Christ came to earth to establish the City of God upon earth. The Kingdom which he proclaimed was bound inseparably to the society which would finally inherit it. In fact he had so trained his followers that they could be the first manifestation of this "new society" and an exemplification of the kind of communal relations that should characterize it. While the initiative rested with Heaven, men were expected by repentance and prayer and obedience to resist social evil and to ready the world so that the law of Christ might be perfectly fulfilled.

His social teachings included the right of every man to call upon God as Father; a recognition of the dignity and worth of each individual; and the inestimable value of man's immortal soul. His own life was a confirmation and acknowledgment of the inalienable rights of a neighbor and a prohibition of every form of oppression. No one dare use his neighbor as a tool to further his own ends. All men constitute a single family with the status of children of the Heavenly Father. And in the light of this, his ministers could scarcely refrain from standing in judgment upon such a denial of Christ as was being exhibited outside Central High School.

73

Another basis of their judgment lay in the belief that the Church, because it is the treasure house of the Gospel, has a special responsibility to society over and above all human institutions, including the state. Under normal conditions the state is entitled to receive the respect and obedience of Christians who are to render unto Caesar the things that are Caesar's. But whenever the state fails to provide the security due to each of its people, then it is the duty of the Church to discharge its God-given function and point out such violations of Christian principle. And the Church has the duty to do this because the state is a human institution composed of finite men, liable to sin and subject to error.

Of course, the statements and debates of the Little Rock Ministerial Alliance were not as specific as the above seems to indicate. However, it does summarize much that was said. The ministers were agreed that the Gospel had something to say to that part of society which lay beyond the membership of their own congregations. They knew they had a duty as Christ's servants, both to point out society's fault and to point to a higher vision. Also, they recognized the need for people within and without their congregations to know what Christ teaches and where the Church stands. All former divisions among them were, therefore, put aside in favor of a strong "thus saith the Lord."

### PASTORAL LETTER

Immediately following the meeting of the Ministerial Alliance that Black Monday, the Little Rock clericus of Episcopal clergymen was convened at Christ Church.

There followed a lengthy discussion concerning the motives of the leaders of the several factions in the desegregation dispute and the consequences of C.C.C. action not only in prompting a mob, but also in exercising an effect upon the students within the school. Out of the discussion two points became apparent. First, a Pastoral Letter from the Bishop was necessary in order to identify the Episcopal Church's position and uphold the hands of the clergy who were facing their congregations and the community as a whole with the Christian judgment. Second, the clergy must be assured of the Bishop's complete support so long as their own pronouncements were given after calm, deliberate thought reached during long periods spent on their knees and not as the result of quixotic, unrealistic, spur-of-the-moment enthusiasm.

When the clergy adjourned, the Bishop prepared what he hoped would serve as a testimony to the Gospel, a spur to Christian conscience and a proper climate for discussion and opinion. Addressing his Pastoral Letter to the Episcopal Churches in Little Rock, he said:

"My dear Friends:

I have hoped and prayed these last two weeks that by some miracle or chance a way might be opened in the Little Rock school situation to bring order out of chaos and peace out of passion. To that end I have tried to work behind the scenes with some leaders to gain the time necessary for such a miracle to work. I refrained from any public statement other than a summary of the Christian faith in the hope of establishing an objectivity for myself which would permit the exercise of a Ministry of Reconciliation among the several disagreeing groups. Perhaps such a hope

75

was vain and foolish. At any rate, it failed dismally.

"This morning at Central High School there was physical violence which cannot for a moment be condoned by any Christian body. It stabs at the heart of churchmen and forces a cry of pain and compassion. In fact, it urges us to our knees in shame over our inability to exert an adequate Christian leadership in this hour. And having attempted every secret remedy known to me without success, now, in view of this violence, I must take my open stand with that of my Church and call upon every loyal Episcopalian to do the same.

"As you know, the Church has declared through its General Convention, the Lambeth Conference, the Anglican Congress, the National Council of the Churches of Christ in the United States of America, and the World Council of Churches, that unjust social discrimination is contrary to the mind of Christ and the will of God. Let me quote only one of these resolutions which was passed by the General Convention as far back as 1952 at its meeting in Boston,

'Whereas Christ teaches above all the Fatherhood of God, the consequent brotherhood of man and the oneness of the whole human family; and

'Whereas, present day developments, leading to an increased interdependence of nations, are making ever clearer the necessity of Christ's way of brotherhood; and

'Whereas, Christ's teaching is incompatible with every form of discrimination based on color or race, both domestic and international; and

'Whereas, almost every country today, including our own, is guilty in greater or lesser degree of mass racial or color discrimination; therefore,

76

'Be it resolved, that we consistently oppose and combat discrimination based on color or race of every form, both within the Church and without, in this country and internationally.'

"To this, and every other such action of the Church, I fully subscribe. The principle offered is nothing more than that of the Son of God. I have also sworn to be ready 'with all faithful diligence, to banish and drive away from the Church all erroneous and strange doctrine contrary to God's word.'

"Therefore, I call upon the clergy, the laymen, the laywomen and the youth of the Episcopal churches in Little Rock:

1. To refrain from every word or deed which is not consistent with the teachings of Jesus Christ concerning the brotherhood of man.
2. To exercise Christian leadership and influence under every public circumstance, especially as regards patience, understanding and Christian love.
3. To offer hourly prayer for God's guidance of our leaders in community, state, and nation.
4. To make a firm resistance against every pressure of an unthinking society.

"This I do in full knowledge that my call may not meet with a ready acceptance on the part of everyone. Yet, when emotion replaces mind, a mob is substituted for law, and violence overrules arbitration; then, under God and as your Bishop, I must do so in the name of Christ.

Faithfully and affectionately yours,
Robert R. Brown,
Bishop of Arkansas"

### THE EFFECTS OF
### THE PASTORAL LETTER

This letter was received by the congregations of the Little Rock Episcopal churches with some taciturnity. The diocesan branch of the Woman's Auxiliary wired an expression of gratitude. The vestry of a nearby parish passed resolutions of appreciation and of prayer. Individual letters and phone calls offering support were received. But there was obvious disagreement in many instances and some misunderstanding of the Pastoral's intent. Rumor had it that the Bishop was going to excommunicate all segregationists, that he didn't really believe in integration himself and was only obeying Church orders, that he was being unduly influenced by the idealistic clergy of Arkansas—but none of this broke out into open antagonism. On first review it appeared that the Church's stand had only created another divisive situation, and increased the chasm between clergy and laity, as well as between Christian Church and secular society. The hushed words of appreciation were sincere, but for the most part the uneasy silence seemed to indicate more sorely what people were really thinking and feeling.

Later it became evident that most of the silence was not the result of personal opposition, but of uneasy self-consciousness. It was difficult to know what to say, hard to carry on normal conversation without saying something, and there was always the ever-present possibility of saying the wrong thing. So with real wisdom Episcopalians said nothing. They did not voice nor write objections which would have put their Bishop on the defensive in his attempts to answer. Neither did they take unequivocal positions from which they could not retreat with honor. They simply let time work for them. Then, slowly, they began to come forward in normal, natural ways. On the whole, this was the best possible response.

It is interesting that during the hottest days of the crisis when Little Rock was receiving national publicity, an average morning's mail brought something in the neighborhood of 50 letters and telegrams about "this situation." Yet of hundreds received, there was only one derogatory letter from an Arkansas Episcopalian. The great bulk of the mail came from outside the state—from North and South in almost equal proportions—and about half of it was congratulatory, the other half critical.

That which accused was resentful of the Church "entering politics." One telegram from Louisiana read, "Please keep our Church out of both sides." An editorial mailed from Mississippi said of Congressman Brooks Hays, "The South is not in a mood to follow [his] namby-pamby leadership . . . even if it does so happen that he is president of the Baptist Southern Convention. Hays favors integration and is, therefore, not a fit leader for Christian people. 'Our mission is to find the common denominator,' says Bishop Brown. There is no common denominator. This is a matter of eternal principles, not a theory in mathematics." Still another bit of correspondence stated that "The Committee on Moderation certainly looks like the Steering Committee for the Republican Party . . . your dive into Arkansas politics is about as free from bias as is John Kasper's position." And from Alabama came the advice, "I sincerely believe that you and other preachers

79

and churches should stick closely to your business of saving souls and stay out of this integration mess. . . . I know of no movement that has gone so far in bringing the preachers and their churches into disrepute than their attempt to destroy the handiwork of God by advocating the mixing of members of the white and colored races. . . ."

On the other hand, a telegram of commendation from New Jersey expressed gratitude to all "the people of good will and their efforts to mobilize the moral and spiritual resources of Little Rock." A letter from an Arkansas college student, an Episcopalian who had graduated from Central High School the preceding June, said: "Last year, when I was a senior representative on the Student Council . . . we were positive of the fact that Central would integrate peacefully and with dignity. The blow given our problem was a shock to the majority of students. I was sick. . . . My reason for writing to you is simple: to thank you. . . . After reading the articles published in *Time,* I knew my worry was over." A seventeen-year-old girl from Nebraska wrote, "Believing in realization of spiritual life and a Christian upholding of God's truth, I pray for the cause of any man and men who shall so live and progress, if ever so little, for the cause of love." A planter from Mississippi said: "Be assured you have my prayers as well as those of many millions of American citizens." Even one of the United Press correspondents wrote before returning to Washington: "As an Episcopal layman who has been covering the ordeal of your city as a news correspondent for the past two weeks, I wanted to record . . . the pride I have felt in all the Episcopal churches in Little Rock."

Such correspondence, of both sorts, is fairly representative, but very little of it came from Arkansas. There certainly was some thoughtless, but insistent, talk that the Church had no authority to speak on such issues, thus implying that Christianity must become subservient to the world. A rather wistful hope was expressed that somehow the Church could sit in the gallery for spectators and watch the conflict without becoming implicated. There was a little querying as to whether the actions of General Convention were binding upon individual Episcopalians or congregations. A few went to Holy Scripture in support of their positions. But most of this could be labeled as "street-corner conversation" which did not cause a rise in temperature or prove embarrassing.

However, it must also be confessed that the Pastoral Letter did not completely perform the task for which it was intended. While it may have pointed up the Church's stand and given some witness to the Gospel, it would be difficult to prove that it was successful in either pricking the conscience of individuals or in leading them to put aside personal preferences in the light of larger issues.

## THE CHURCH'S RIGHT TO SPEAK

The task the Little Rock clergy found most discouraging —that of earning the right to speak and to be heard on the social issues of life—points up a major task of the Church. Most ministers realize, in an academic, impersonal way, that the Church has always had great difficulty in exercising influence upon leaders involved with the burning issues of life. Now in a more personal manner they have been brought to understand, sadly, that their urgent calls to repent from "riotous living" are going unheard because their people are not really recognizing the appalling power of sin, nor agreeing that repentance on their part is necessary. Pastoral counselling should have given these ministers some insight into the numbers who have not yet seen themselves in the mirror of Christ. The casualness with which these people accept the pragmatic values of the business and social world should have warned them that the ministry was looked upon as something of an anachronism. The astounding unawareness of the people in the pews—not to mention that of the man in the street—concerning the elementary aspects of the Faith should have served notice that these people would not follow where their more spiritually experienced pastors were endeavoring to lead them. But it took the crisis here in Little Rock to make all these points and to cause them to admit the staggering conclusion that as clergymen they were largely without influence in the time of trouble.

They were well enough aware of the indictment this fact leveled against them. They openly avowed the need for repentance and forgiveness. But this did not alleviate the pain experienced when they found themselves crying out to a society that would not listen. What they were proclaiming as sacred, many of their own church members rejected as impractical and unrealistic. What they witnessed as the Gospel, the average man would not accept. What they insisted was truth, not a few disavowed as moralism and sentimentality.

The story is told of a politician who, in lining up some candidates for public office, called in a few of his henchmen for suggestions of community organizations to endorse the candidates. When one such organization was mentioned, the politician shuddered and said, "Hell no, that would be as bad as being endorsed by the Ministerial Union." The Rev. Colbert S. Cartwright, in an article in the *Christian Century* (Oct. 9, 1957), verifies this story's truth by stating that when the Little Rock Ministerial Alliance approached Mr. Virgil Blossom, the Superintendent of Schools, with an offer to endorse the Little Rock Plan of desegregation, Mr. Blossom begged the ministers *not* to endorse this plan, either officially or publicly.

Certainly the clergy had erred, as they will be the first to admit, having manifested too often a concern for lesser things which limited their vision. Certainly the divisive elements in denominationalism split their united strength and give the world an impression of weakness. Furthermore, they do not always recognize the vast distance that exists between altar, pulpit, and pew. Therefore, they expect far more of the laity than it is capable of producing. As one clergyman said at a meeting on desegregation, "I was born and raised in the South and imbued with all the Southern prejudices. It took my conversion to Christ, my ordination and many years in the ministry before I could rise above these prejudices. I cannot, therefore, expect my people to change over night." All of these facts, and many more, may have weakened the voice of the preacher in this day, but they should not have stilled it. The clergy and what they represent should be receiving something more than tip-of-the-hat respect such as the world grants to a gentle old man who may have been effective in his youth, but has nothing basic to contribute to life in his last years.

Not that the Little Rock clergy or the churches they represent were anxious to establish some new Church-State relationship that would give them an official, political authority. The separation of Church and State found unanimous agreement with them. The authority they sought and still seek, while admitting their own responsibility in partially losing it, concerns the spiritual and eternal truths. They wanted the hearing that should be given when the things of the Spirit are applied to the temporal problems of life. They felt that the Gospel of Christ had something practical and realistic to say to the society in which they lived and they wanted the right to say it—and to be heard.

But that was the trouble. If the clergy were at fault in failing to command a hearing, the lifelong church members also failed to interpret properly the staggering implications of what had been taught and preached over and over again. They reserved the right to make a cafeteria approach to the Gospel, to pick and choose according to their personal inclinations. They exercised the privilege of making their own biblical exegesis and expositions apart from the more learned interpretations. In no few instances they also mistook the minister for his message and condemned him personally for his temerity in presenting that which is specifically the content of the Gospel. And, too regularly, they preferred to think that the prophetic application should be directed to someone else, but never to themselves. They did not see the accusing finger of Christ leveled at them individually, nor did they hear the implied words "This means you!"

Had the lifelong church members been aware of the Christian principles involved; had they been obedient, not to the clergy but to the Gospel; there would have been raised up in Little Rock such a cry as would have forced public leadership to give credence to it. But this did not happen.

On one occasion, a church leader appearing before a body of men with some official responsibility for breaking the deadlock between the contending forces, told them almost in a spirit of exasperation: "Gentlemen, I would remind you that the clergy of the city represent not an inconsiderable body of people who want this impasse solved and they all have votes." That body remained unmoved. It knew the Church posed no political threat—and so did the clergymen whose bluff was called.

The fact remains that the followers of the Christ who came to earth for all sorts and conditions of men, who consorted with such untouchables as Samaritans and Publicans, who died as much for those who placed him on the Cross as for those who knelt beneath it, have not yet succeeded in permitting him to make his impact upon their everyday lives. Neither have they remembered such early Church traditions as Philip's relation to the Ethiopian, or Paul's to the Greek and the Jew, the circumcised and the uncircumcised, the barbarian, the Scythian, the slave and the free, nor related them to their prejudices and insecurities. There was the same human failure to see the Christ as the goal of what all men ought to be and as the Perfect Reality against which they have rebelled. Thus, they had neither been brought down to their knees in repentance and remorse, nor raised up with courage and determination to witness to the life of their Lord.

This division between the pulpit and the pew, and the consequent inability of the Church to affect a strong moral pressure upon what is actually a series of moral problems, is perhaps the most damaging weakness of all. It is not confined to Little Rock, of course. Ministers of all faiths in Atlanta, Richmond and Charleston—and, for that matter, in Brooklyn, Detroit and Cincinnati—have spoken and written of it. But granted the failure of the clergy and laity alike, how can the matter be rectified in the future? What can be done, by God's grace, which will assist the Church to confront society with both judgment and reconciliation? These are questions which make this whole issue bigger than Little Rock.

In summary, then, it seems safe to describe the Church's condition in Little Rock and elsewhere as *not* "one Body we." The divisive interpretations at work between the various communions, between the ministers themselves, and between them and their people have undermined the spiritual unity and moral force which should have been brought to bear. This is not to imply that the Church did nothing. As we have seen, and shall see in succeeding chapters, church leaders worked heroically with their congregations and with their community in spite of these weaknesses—or, perhaps, because of them.

But there lingers the sad thought of what might have been.

# 5

# THE MINISTRY

# OF

# RECONCILIATION

At all times and in all places, the Christian Church must
—despite secular apathy and indifference—exercise its
right to stand in judgment upon whatever is amiss in the
society to which it has been sent. No matter how deaf an
ear the world may turn to the Gospel or how competitive
the voices it may raise to drown that message, the mes-
sengers of Christ must still bear witness to justice and point
the stern finger of accusation at every form of bias and un-
righteousness.

Yet, as fundamental as this fact is, it is never enough in

itself. The accusing finger condemns, but it does not heal. It is like holding a mirror up to a small boy to show him that his face is dirty, without providing soap, water, and a washcloth. Or, to switch to metaphor, judgment is the sharp ax which hacks away at the faults of man; but it must not be used without that healing balm which is the remedy for the wounds of his sin and the means of attaining moral health. Judgment accuses—it also divides and can destroy. Like surgery, it is a necessary process—but what surgeon operates and then abandons his patient? And the mission of the Church to the world is both to judge and to heal, or it is no mission at all.

*God was in Christ, reconciling the world unto himself . . . and hath committed unto us the word of reconciliation.* These few words from St. Paul reveal the purpose of God for his creation, the meaning of the life of Christ, and the task of his Church. In the exercise of its ministry the Church holds fast to these words as the mandate for all its activity as a redeeming agent in the world. St. Paul is quite definite about the fact that the Church is the "Body" of Christ through which God acts as he did in Christ; that the Church, like its Lord, girt *with the whole armour of God,* must stand in the evil day. And St. Paul is quite definite about the consequences of this fact. For Christ it meant the Cross which saved us from our own devices and placed us within the realm of redemption. For the Church it may mean persecution, rejection, and indifference. But however the world regards the voice of the Church, the Church must sustain the dynamic tension of its twofold mission. For, what God must judge and punish he must also win to himself in love. Like the child of a loving parent, man has to learn to accept rebuke given out of love and concern. And it is within the framework of this eternal dialogue of God with man *through the Church* that reconciliation is effected and redemption made sure.

## THE CLERGY CONSIDER NEXT STEPS

Firm in the conviction of their mission, and having made their judgment upon violence and discrimination, the clergy of Little Rock proceeded to a prayerful consideration of the next necessary steps. What Christ wants, and what the Church must strive for, is not separation but transformation and restoration—reconciliation. And so, having individually and collectively witnessed to justice, these ministers were concerned next to witness corporately to love. Having spoken the truth in love, it was also necessary, in that same love, for them to offer mediation. To fix blame for the crisis was not important—history could do that in its own good time. What was important was to hold up the goal of a Christian society; and to accomplish that, affirmative action was required. They had good biblical authority for such a decision which would in no wise minimize, or imply retreat from, their previous moral judgments. Did not the Christ condemn the "blind leaders of the blind" and still cry, *Father, forgive them for they know not what they do?* Surely love and forgiveness, not condemnation, lie at the heart of the Gospel.

The ministers of Little Rock knew they could not command love. Respect, perhaps, or fear, but not love. They were also aware of their failure to lead society into the way of love. When they had attempted that, they had been met with apathy and even insult. But at least they could

89

witness love by their own example and pray that their witness would inspire a response. This was the motive behind their next action. In some areas it was interpreted as a retreat from their original position. In others it was considered a weak, sentimental approach to a problem that required robust handling. Some of the clergy were not certain but that a strong moral pronouncement might obtain better results. But the large majority agreed that judgment having been made on justice, it was important now that this judging stand under the higher judgment of Christian love.

## THE DOCTRINE OF RECONCILIATION

Repentance and a confessed humility entered their discussion yet again at this point. The citizens of Little Rock needed to see that the sternness of previous pronouncements did not come from a group who felt themselves "holier than thou." Average churchmen must be led to understand that, in preaching obedience to the Gospel, their ministers were not cutting themselves off from their congregations or refusing to recognize their own involvement in a corporate sin. The reason for their repentance was not only the failures of their weakened leadership, but also the stark realization that they were as bound up in the Little Rock crisis and as much a part of the society that made possible the assembling of the mob at Central High School as any of their people. The sack cloth and ashes with which they draped their hearts were real. And as the clergyman comes down from the chancel and joins the congregation for the reading of the Litany, so the Little Rock clergy desired to join with their congregations in a common

90

confession of a common sin. This, they were convinced, was the point at which they must begin the exercise of their Ministry of Reconciliation.

The goal of this Ministry was to reopen all lines of communication through love. To speak briefly in theological terms, the Ministry of Reconciliation is the witness of Man's reconciliation with God. Its purpose is to teach that the Heavenly Father sent his Son to earth to reconcile the world unto himself and that, in giving of himself on a cross, the Son set into operation a grace which flowed from him unto his followers, offering forgiveness, deliverance from sin, and the opening of Heaven's gates. The initiative is God's, the gift is God's; man's chief responsibility is to know that he is *already* reconciled and, accordingly, expected to respond as a child of God and a brother to man. Reconciliation which began as a downward, vertical thrust from Heaven has continued as the outward horizontal reach of redeemed men to their neighbors. The two cannot be separated, for they comprise a mutual interaction of love. Neither can man be a brother to his fellowman without this grace of God's reconciliation for the simple reason that his selfish nature will not permit him to be one. Thus, while the immediate goal of the Little Rock ministers was to reopen the lines of communication between men, they were also well aware that this could not be achieved apart from the basic spiritual purpose of reopening the lines of communication with God. How should they proceed in this? Being without political influence or the power to persuade, they were thrust back upon the even more vital witness of a personal Christian love.

## FINDING A PROGRAM

Meanwhile, however, a friend in the State Department had been asked how the Church might implement its witness and play its Christian part in the crisis. A few days later a letter was received from President Eisenhower, expressing the belief that there was much the Little Rock ministers could do to place matters in their proper perspective. In part the letter said: "The founders of our nation clearly felt that free government is a political expression of religious faith, with basic human rights deriving directly from the individual's Creator. Religious leaders have an especial opportunity, I think, to help keep such a government strong and vital and continuously devoted to the concepts that inspired the signers of the Declaration of Independence." Concerning the violence at Central High School, the President continued: "The immediate question is not at all whether any particular individual agrees with a particular decision of the Supreme Court. The real question is whether we shall respect the institutions of free government or, by defying them, set up either a process of deterioration and disruption or compel the authorities to resort to force to obtain that respect which we all should willingly give."

The letter stated in conclusion: "All of us realize that not through legislation alone can prejudice and hatred be eliminated from the hearts of men. Leadership, including religious leadership, must play its part. . . . I am convinced that if all of us work together, that in the spirit implicit in your suggestion, we should eventually be able to work out all our problems, including those of race, and

92

as a consequence, our beloved country will be greater, stronger and more secure in all the years to come."

On receipt of this correspondence a group of Little Rock ministers convened to discuss the Church's place in the school crisis. The meeting was attended by Dr. Aubrey Walton of the First Methodist Church; Dr. Marion Boggs, pastor of the Second Presbyterian Church; the Rev. Dunbar Ogden, Jr., pastor of the Central Presbyterian Church and president of the Ministerial Alliance; Rabbi Ira Sanders of Temple B'nai Israel; Congressman Brooks Hays, president of the Southern Baptist Convention; and the writer. The Most Rev. Albert L. Fletcher, Roman Catholic bishop of the Diocese of Little Rock, and Dr. W. O. Vaught, Jr., pastor of Emmanuel Baptist Church, were, unfortunately, out of the city, as was Bishop Paul E. Martin of the Methodist Church.

It was at this preliminary meeting that their thinking about the Ministry of Reconciliation began to crystallize. The proposal was made that the clergy of the city be invited to a Conference at Trinity Cathedral to consider the feasibility of a city-wide day of prayer and that these services be followed by the organization of small groups to discuss the Christian implications of the desegregation program in such an atmosphere as obtains when two or three are gathered together in Christ's name. It was agreed, first of all, that each congregation should conduct its own prayer service according to its rites and ceremonies. In this way the people could feel more comfortable with their familiar form of worship, and each denomination could participate in a way impossible at a larger mass meeting. It was believed, further, that at this point, only

93

the ministers of white congregations should receive invitations to the Cathedral Conference. First, because the mere presence of Negro clergy might at this preliminary stage increase the tensions and make impossible uninhibited discussion of the proposal. Second, because the desegregation problem was in fact chiefly one for the white congregations to solve. It was understood, however, that an explanation of this decision should be given to the pastors of the Negro churches and that they and their congregations would be invited wholeheartedly to participate if the proposal was accepted by the white clergy. It was for these reasons that invitations to the ministers were sent from the Bishop of Arkansas rather than from the Ministerial Alliance. The Negro clergy were quite understanding of this procedure and promised a readiness to cooperate at the proper time.

Two other suggestions grew out of this smaller meeting. First, that the city-wide Day of Prayer be held on Columbus Day, October 12. Second, that the Governor of Arkansas and the Little Rock School Board should be advised of the proposal.

When the Governor was approached, he signified immediately his own desire to address a letter to the clergy of Little Rock endorsing the program. In this letter he said: "We deeply deplore the occurrences in our capital city of recent days . . . your attitude of seeking to bring about reconciliation, rather than attempting to place blame, is, I believe, the proper approach at this time. . . . It is not a time now for recrimination or blame-placing. It is a time for sober, sensible reflection, with a humble and prayerful approach. . . . We must face the fact that this is not a

94

situation which will yield readily to a solution. It will take time, patience, understanding, and prayer. . . . In your efforts of reconciliation, you shall have my understanding and full support. Realizing the difficulties which you face, and which we all face, it is my prayer that God will give you understanding and the wisdom to proceed with courage, with faith, with tolerance, and understanding."

The Superintendent of Schools and members of the School Board were also ready to endorse the program. A letter signed by Dr. W. G. Cooper, Jr., president of the Little Rock Board of Education, and by Virgil T. Blossom, the Superintendent, said: "The Little Rock Board of Education, in all humbleness and sincerity, would like to join with the President of our country and the Governor of our State in asking the people of Little Rock to pray for divine guidance for the leaders of our community, of our State, and of our nation; and for each and everyone of us concerned in this serious and far-reaching crisis we are now facing. May we find it in our hearts to be united before God in that we will unfailingly and tirelessly and humbly beseech his guidance in the present situation in order that the best, not the worst, may come out in all of us. Law and order must, for all concerned, be vigorously maintained."

## THE CLERGY RALLY

It seemed to the clergy that here, finally, was a degree of unity. Although in marked disagreement over the principles and procedures of desegregation, the President of the United States, the Governor of Arkansas, and the Little Rock School Board agreed completely in the need for humility, the guidance of God and the necessity of prayer and discussion. Whatever else separated them, they joined together on this, and it was felt that at last there was a spiritual unanimity among these leaders which could lead the people to mutual objectivity, understanding, and peace.

The Cathedral Conference was called on October 4, and some forty white clergymen responded. The three letters were read and the program for the Ministry of Reconciliation, as it applied to the crisis, was proposed. The truth emphasized was that regardless of existing disagreements, there is always some room for Christian love.

Bishop Paul Martin of the Methodist Church was present, having returned from Europe and Africa only a few days previously. He said: "This is a day in which men must submerge their passions and their prejudices for the sake of the greater cause—the Brotherhood of Man under the Fatherhood of God." Continuing, he said, "I do not know what will be the final answer. I know this will be resolved. It cannot help but be resolved. I do not have the answer . . . but there is an answer under God. . . . under the leadership of the Holy Spirit there will come again to our fair land that which will bless all of humanity."

Monsignor James E. O'Connell, representing Bishop Fletcher, added: "I can assure all of you that the Roman Catholic Church will be pleased to cooperate with all of you as these proposals suggest we cooperate. . . . I am convinced, as I know all of you dedicated men must be, that with prayer we can accomplish wonders. . . . The Catholic people in this community and throughout the state will be with you in this great spiritual effort to cast out the devils of prejudice and violence."

Rabbi Ira Sanders continued: "If ever there was a time

when we ministers are called upon to reaffirm the dignity of the individual to which all faiths in the world subscribe, that time has come. . . . By means of prayer we should fulfill our Ministry of Reconciliation with God and our fellowmen. And so I am happy that we can use the synagogue on Columbus Day. And I, as the Rabbi of the synagogue, wish to reaffirm, first, the dignity of the individual and, secondly . . . justice for all people, of all races, and all creeds."

"It seems to me that the time has come for us to exercise this Ministry of Reconciliation," said Dr. Marion Boggs. "I like the idea of having services all at the same time. I'd like the idea of each denomination or each pastor having his own people at such a service. It will give me an opportunity to put the pastoral arm around men in my congregation who have difficulties in going with us in our conviction and judgment. It will give me an opportunity as a pastor to bring back close into the fellowship of the Church those who feel that something has been expressed in which they cannot fully agree. So I want to express myself in hearty agreement with the program that has been outlined."

Such statements were representative of the thought that prevailed, and the Cathedral Conference concluded—only one dissenting—with the decision to invite the citizens of Little Rock to join in Columbus Day services of prayer for:

1. Forgiveness for having left undone the things we ought to have done.
2. The support and preservation of law and order.
3. The leaders of our community, state and nation.
4. The youth in the schools of our community.

5. The casting out of rancor and prejudice in favor of understanding and compassion.

6. Resistance against unthinking agitators.

The clergy departed from the conference with a feeling of accomplishment and unanimity.

Dissenters did arise, however. A group of twenty-four Baptist ministers of the more fundamentalistic persuasion called a similar worship service for the evening preceding. They invited their people to pray: "(1) For our national leaders. That they be guided by constitutional law rather than by politics. (2) For our state leaders. That they be given the wisdom and the courage to fulfill their responsibilities to the citizens of the State of Arkansas. (3) For all citizens. That under these trying circumstances, no overt acts be performed for which we would be sorry later."

The spokesman of this group explained that they could not participate in the Columbus Day observance because "Jews, Catholics and Protestants were taking part in it." "Jews," he said, "do not believe in the Deity of the Lord Jesus Christ. Catholics, while believing in the Lord Jesus Christ, pray through the Virgin Mary. Most of the Protestants involved in the call are of the modernistic persuasion. Modernists do not believe in the Virgin Birth or the Deity of the Lord Jesus Christ." The service held by this group, however, emphasized a segregationist point of view. This, of course, proved confusing to many who were made to feel two rival camps were being organized to petition God.

Then, the League of Central High Mothers placed a quarter page advertisement in one of the newspapers, addressed "To the Clergymen, Catholic, Jewish and Protestant, who are promoting the Prayer Meetings Saturday,

98

October 12, for the purpose of restoring peace and tranquility to our community." The advertisement made the following statements under the guise of questions:

"You preachers who are planning this crusade are well-known. Your activities toward race-mixing are well-known. For years you have agitated the integration of our schools. Now that the issue is hot, you do not discuss the question on its merits and flee to the 'law of the land' argument. Why not admit you are for race-mixing and fight the battle out on its merits? . . . Do we have a right to ask God to do for us what we can do for ourselves? You are asking God to heal our city. If the Negro children were in their own schools, our city would be peaceful again. How can you advocate race-mixing and pray to escape the fruits of race-mixing? Is it proper for those who have for years advocated race-mixing to come forward as peacemakers? Are the ones whose philosophy created the problem the proper ones to prescribe the remedy?"

### THE MINISTRY OF RECONCILIATION

Thus the Ministry of Reconciliation also created disagreement and opposition from the beginning. Perhaps this was to be expected for the term "Ministry of Reconciliation," though well-known and understood by the clergy, was unfamiliar to the people of Little Rock, and to the newspaper correspondents reporting the program. Misunderstanding persisted, although the scriptural authority for this Ministry was carefully cited from St. Paul, both in II Corinthians, *And all things are of God, who hath reconciled us to himself by Jesus Christ, and hath given to us the ministry of reconciliation,* and from Ephesians how Christ's

Atonement *hath broken down the middle wall of partition between us.* These verses were explained and still again it was stated that such a Ministry should not be interpreted as a retreat from the Christian judgment already given. Special emphasis was placed on the initiative of Christ in breaking down *the middle wall of partition.* However, there was misunderstanding and no little misinterpretation according to personal prejudice.

Some misconceived the Ministry of Reconciliation as "conciliation." They took the word in its sense of inferring weakness; as, for instance, gaining goodwill; appeasing for private benefit; or placating because of an anxiety for security. It seemed to them that, protestations to the contrary, the clergy were retreating from their former positions and attempting to compromise at any cost. This, they said, was a bit of cowardice which proved the clergy had been wrong in the first place and were now confessing it. It was considered an intolerable attempt on the part of the clergy to kiss the hand that had struck them.

Others interpreted "reconciliation" as the accepting of a condition in passive resignation; as compliance and the adaptation of one's self with resignation to a situation in which one is helpless. This notion exasperated them, for it was not the American way to submit to indignity without attempting to defend oneself. Whatever else Arkansans may be, they are not a people to remain submissive to a condition they do not approve. So, here again, a false interpretation of the Christian Ministry of Reconciliation led some citizens of Little Rock far astray from the true, theological purpose.

In fact, it is questionable whether, even with explanation,

very many really saw this approach in its New Testament context. They did not recognize its source in God's initiative or in the Christ, who through his life, death and resurrection brought reconciliation between man and God and between man and man. Nor did they understand the Christian contention that this Ministry was an attempt at the *spiritual* restoration of man from enmity and estrangement with his brother. To a great number, any effort to bridge the gap between diverse opinions or to draw men to open their minds, calm their passions, and restore the lines of communications with one another, was a sign of vassalage. They simply could not see that it was possible to express love without the sacrifice of principle. Nor could they recognize the impossibility of reaping the valid fruits of Christian ethics either in the life of individuals or in society as a whole, apart from the seeds of reconciliation between God and man.

In view of such misunderstanding perhaps the use of the phrase was ill-advised. Possibly it would have been better to have spoken with less scriptural authority and in secular terms understandable to the average citizen. Yet, even now it is difficult to pick a word or phrase which would not have been subjected to the same mistaken interpretations or used as ammunition for the same accusations. The semantic problem and the lack of understanding rested probably, in large part, upon the clergy's inability to explain clearly what was meant by the Ministry of Reconciliation. Yet despite this failure, there was sufficiently common ground within the program of this Ministry on which people could, and did, meet.

One example of this was the fact that the President, the

Governor, and the School Board, all joined in looking to
the Church for leadership. In spite of accusations that they
all wanted the ministers to serve some political purpose,
or "to pull their chestnuts out of the fire for them," there
is no reason to believe that they were not completely
sincere. It was not naïveté to accept at face value their
requests for prayer and guidance, as well as their expressed
desires for a way out of their impasse. And while some were
suspicious and others, according to their position, inclined
to remember only one of the letters to the neglect of the
others, a great many people felt that here was a juncture
where all factions, including their own, could meet.

Again, there was an almost intense desire on the part
of many to play some part in solving the problem. As one
lady expressed it, "We little people want the opportunity
to be seen and heard." Several church members came
forward with the same suggestion that a mass prayer service
be held, and it was their request which led finally to the
Day of Prayer on Columbus Day. To such as these, the
opportunity for public worship was like a plebiscite which
afforded them the right to cast their prayers for peace and
order and goodwill. These people were not members of the
groups that had mushroomed up to lobby or exert pressure in favor of a particular viewpoint, nor were they
among those who were filling the "Letters to the Editor"
columns in the newspapers with emotional outbursts. These
were the "moderates," whom all parties claimed to represent, yet who had been given no opportunity to express
their point of view.

By this time, there was general embarrassment in the
community over the notoriety Little Rock was receiving

from the press all over the world. Much of that publicity made the citizens of the community appear to be illiterate, backward, gun-carrying mobsters, with no concern for government or civilization. It caused letters by the thousands to be addressed here with the same prejudiced questions: "What are you people like in Arkansas?" "What do you expect to accomplish?" The average resident of Little Rock resented this blanket judgment of the world as totally unfair and was concerned to prove by some action that he was not to be identified with the mob that had gathered outside the High School. He wanted to show that the agitators were not a representative group and that Little Rock is truly an average American city.

And, too, there was a general desire that the impasse between the President, the Governor, and the School Board, which had now existed for a month be in some way solved. The extremists had taken their stand and were crying "no quarter." Their belligerent shot-gun approach, scattering blasts in all directions, had put the moderates on the defensive, forcing them either to remain silent or to spend their time defending themselves against these attacks, instead of going on the offensive. The Day of Prayer now offered a Christian offensive to those who wanted to play a part in this movement which was, in some ways, one of passive resistance and to show that there were *seven thousand others who had not bowed the knee to Baal.*

### THE DAY OF PRAYER

These common desires when joined with the fundamental belief in the power of prayer formed a happy combination. On October 12, the people flocked to their churches. No telephone calls or pamphlets or other special methods were used to encourage public attendance. And, although this was a Saturday morning with children home from school, week-end programs to be arranged, shopping to be done, and all the other competitions normal to a Saturday, between eight and ten thousand citizens of Little Rock attended these services. Church bells rang over the city. Some stores closed completely, many gave their employees time off to attend services, and a few held a minute of silence at eleven o'clock.

It is difficult to give the exact number of worshippers or of congregations which participated, for many churches did not report their services, others never reported the attendance. The advertisement carried in the papers the day before listed eighty congregations, but many others have called in since that time to say that they had cooperated also, and it is certain that a minimum of eighty-six churches were represented. A breakdown by denomination shows that among the participants were at least 12 Baptist churches, 27 Methodist churches, 7 Presbyterian churches, the 2 Jewish synagogues, all the Episcopal churches, and all the Roman Catholic churches. Also participating were the Greek Orthodox, Disciples of Christ, the Lutherans, The Church of the Nazarene, the Salvation Army, and not a few community chapels.

In some instances, the Holy Communion or the Roman Catholic Mass was celebrated, in others the Litany was read, and in still others sermons were preached; but in all the services, prayers for forgiveness, for the guidance of leaders and the preservation of youth, for the support of law and protection against prejudice were offered. It was a solemn

104

hour in Little Rock. Aside from those who were actually in church at the time, later information indicates that there were thousands more who, having clipped the newspaper advertisements listing the subjects for intercession, offered their prayers at home or office, or even in automobiles as they were journeying to other communities for business or social reasons.

Another warm encouragement came from various church organizations over the state and nation indicating that they were joining in prayer with the people of Little Rock on the same date and at the same time. A great many communities and individual churches held services throughout Arkansas: in Hot Springs and Hope; in Batesville and Benton; in Lonake and Scott and Carlisle and Conway; in Fayetteville and Harrison and Fort Smith and Pine Bluff— to name only a few. Most of the Episcopal churches of the Diocese cooperated and nearly a hundred letters from Episcopal churches in the nation indicated that they, too, were having special services.

Dr. Eugene Carson Blake, President of the National Council of the Churches of Christ, wired: "I believe I represent the prevailing opinion of the people of our constituency and many others of goodwill in expressing to you and others concerned profound gratitude for your call to prayer. . . . I am asking our churches across the country to follow your lead. . . . I am calling attention to the fact that you represent religious groups of all faiths and races and to the objects of prayer as stated by you."

Rabbi Maurice N. Eisendrath, President of the Union of American Hebrew Congregations, stated in his wire: "I am going to recommend to the National Board of the

Union of American Hebrew Congregations . . . to urge efforts similar to yours in communities throughout the nations, both North and South. May God's richest blessings attend you and your colleagues in your vivid demonstration. . . ."

Individual church leaders of other denominations received similar communications from their headquarters. The National Council of the Episcopal Church, for example, said, "We are joining our cause with yours and those of your associates. May God bless you always." The San Diego County Council wired: "The Men's Commission . . . joined the community in Little Rock in offering our prayers for God's guidance and direction in the solution of the grievous problem which confronts you." The Church Federation of Greater Indianapolis said, "Leaders of our churches join you in prayer tomorrow [Columbus Day] for your community and for our beloved country." There were a large number of similar encouragements which made October 12, a national Day of Repentance and Prayer.

It is, of course, impossible to assess the spiritual benefits from this Day of Prayer involving thousands of people over the nation, but certain immediate results seemed to be noticeable in Little Rock. To many—and we hope the wish did not father the observation—there appeared to be a marked lessening of tension after Columbus Day. Perhaps it was only coincidence, but the withdrawal of a large number of the troops guarding Central High School seemed to relate itself to the program of Reconciliation. Then, too, people were less inhibited and more willing to come out in the open and witness their belief in law and order. And certainly, the Day of Prayer had meant a great deal to many individuals who felt helped by the prayer and encouraged by the numbers who had participated in it.

## RECONCILIATION THROUGH DISCUSSION

The second step in the program of the Ministry of Reconciliation called for open-minded discussion. This objective exchange of ideas was planned for small groups of some ten members, and to take place at the local level of the congregation within an atmosphere of Christian faith and love. It was carefully pointed out in advance that discussion is not debate or argument, and is not held for the sake of individual vocal exchange in defense of one's own position. Taking our lead from the text *Where two or three are gathered together in my name, there am I in the midst of them,* we hoped, in the discussion planned, to find the truth in this basic spiritual context.

Everyone in Little Rock still had his personal convictions about the issues involved—or, at least, strong opinions. It seemed, therefore, that intelligent, calm Christian people, by exchanging their points of view, could actually come upon God's truth. This procedure may appear to over-emphasize the Hegelian principle of thesis, antithesis, synthesis, but it was chosen to provide a means to that balance between glorifying one's differences and ignoring them. If God gives man a mind and the freedom to exercise choice, if he grants humanity the ability to see and understand a little of his self-revelation; then, obviously, he intends that the intellect should be brought to bear on the social problems of an age and that the arena should not be left to the emotions alone.

107

It was felt, further, that such discussion should take place within a spiritual atmosphere because more was at stake here than mere fact-finding on a sociological problem. The program called for a religious discussion of a socio-religious issue. It was to proceed under the shadow, and with the guidance, of God. The mere "togetherness" of the group would, it was hoped, become a Fellowship of the Holy Spirit. No matter what the diversity of opinion might be, if there was a unity in Christ, a common concern to find the answer through him, and the inclination to seek for it with Christ-like love, then these many, small discussion cells could give light to an entire community.

It must be understood that this part of the program of the Ministry of Reconciliation has been a much slower process and a far less dramatic one than the first part. After the corporateness of the Columbus Day observance, the clergy had to go back to their own congregations and organize these groups. They were not everywhere successful. Some minds were still so firmly locked in prejudice that it was not possible always to find the right people to make the right beginning. In some instances the clergy did not feel the time was yet propitious for this second step of reconciliation. In one or two instances they were even strongly advised not to attempt it.

Yet the total picture is far from dark. Only now is the work of these groups beginning to bear fruit. From several of them is coming a stouter conviction that Christians must take their stand in spite of any individual prejudice against them and the possibility of their being economically or socially boycotted. In other groups ways and means for breaking the present deadlock between the various areas of disagreement are being considered. In still others, plans are being made whereby "moderates" can become more affirmative and less defensive. Some of these groups cut across denominational boundaries. Some incorporate members of two or three congregations in the same denomination. Now and then there is a large "off-the-record" meeting with formal addresses, or panels with a question and answer period. What the future will reveal about the success of this method, no one now knows. But one fact is certain: Where the motive has been sincere and the approach kept within the proper spiritual framework, the power of Christ's presence has made each member aware that he is already reconciled to God and that he must witness this fact in his daily life in all his relations with his brother.

In summary, let it be said, the clergy of the Little Rock Ministerial Alliance still believe that only a Ministry of Reconciliation offers hope. The conclusion of their program is not yet written. When it is, it will be far more apparent where the churches failed and where they succeeded. Meanwhile, the ministers are not ready to forsake their Witness of Love. Misunderstood though it may be, it still has the authority of Holy Scripture and the promise of peace.

# 6

## COERCION
## AND
## RECONCILIATION

Following the Day of Prayer in October, Little Rock witnessed, as we have noted, an observable lessening of civic tension and an increase of frankness in discussing the integration issue, but no program of action was begun. The elected representatives with direct responsibility in the crisis continued, for whatever reasons, in their refusal to mediate. And individual citizens, with equal persistence, avoided every opportunity to become involved personally. It was obvious by now, however, that the great majority of the people of Little Rock joined with their church leaders

110

in the latter's dissatisfaction with the elected representatives' failure to exercise any initiative in the impasse that had been reached.

The aggressive elements in the community, on the other hand, continued in their defiant course of dividing the population, and thus in maintaining the stalemate. They continued to pursue their program without opposition, while others appeared unwilling to resist with some opposing action. The situation made it imperative that the civil authorities take some action; and the question how to induce them to do this became a very real one.

## THE SCHOOL BOARD PETITIONS THE COURT

Then on February 20, 1958, the Little Rock School Board again petitioned the United States District Court for a postponement of desegregation in its public schools. The plea asked for delay until the phrase, "with all deliberate speed," could be defined more clearly, and specific legal procedures be drawn by which schools could desegregate without impairing the quality of their educational programs. The future judgment of the Court cannot be prophesied, but the petition's description of events portraying the gradual increase of segregationst defiance of the Supreme Court's ruling in 1954 and confessing the School Board's unsuccessful efforts to carry on a satisfactory program of education in an atmosphere of turmoil and confusion, stand as an indictment against public authorities and private citizens alike.

The School Board petition attributed the present impossible state of affairs to these factors:

1. "The Federal Government, except for having placed troops around the school grounds, apparently is powerless to enforce compliance with the court's order of integration and to suppress the interference now being encountered by the officials of the [school] District. Federal officials have not applied penal sanctions to any of the persons who formed into groups near the school grounds, defied the court's order, and interfered with the plan of integration therein specified. They have stepped aside and placed on the [school] District the full responsibility of compliance.

2. "The Judicial Branch of the Federal Government has not aided the District by preventing or attempting to prevent interference with the plan which the officials of the District in a sense of duty, are endeavoring to apply in the operation of the schools within the District.

3. "There has been no effort on the part of the Congress of the United States to strengthen the old, or provide new, judicial procedures which will guarantee enforcement of the civil rights of the Negro minority.

4. "The District, in its respect for the law of the land, is left standing alone, the victim of extraordinary opposition on the part of the State Government and apathy on the part of the Federal Government."

## THE CLERGY DISCUSS A BASIC ISSUE

To a degree, the clergy of Little Rock had anticipated this action. For months previous to the action, each of these objections had been a subject of grave study and had faced

112

the clergy with pertinent, though hypothetical, questions concerning the perplexing relation of *coercion* to *reconciliation*. If the authorized agencies for enforcement were not exercising their power to solve the city's deadlock, should private citizens working through church channels be responsible for doing so? It was perfectly clear to the clergy, however, that while men may coerce agreement through fear, or perhaps even through respect, they cannot force love—and that, therefore, reconciliation could not be forced.

If, then, reconciliation could not be forced, there remained to be faced the stubborn fact of the impasse and the citizen apathy to it. Several questions were, therefore, in order: Should moral and social constraint play a role in the Christian program of preparing a climate for the reconciliation that must eventually come? Should the lion and the tiger be brought through pressure into the ring together in the hope that circumstances would create a certain compatibility and perhaps bring eventual reconciliation? The clergy of Little Rock were particularly sensitive to this possibility, remembering, as they did, Edmund Burke's remark: "There is a limit at which forbearance ceases to be a virtue."

None of the proposals that grew out of these discussions was adopted by the Ministerial Alliance. In one instance, there was no time to introduce the plan and carry it to a successful conclusion; in another, it seemed unlikely that the necessary cooperation could be obtained; in still another, the personal risk to those asked to participate seemed to be too great. Each of the proposals possessed certain moral and spiritual values, and each had a practical aspect as well.

In the final analysis, however, there was always the perplexing and complex question: What is the place of coercion in Christian love? Individual religious leaders struggled with this question in many forms, such as "Does the Church really belong in this field?" "Is this the responsibility of the Ministerial Alliance?" "What are the Christian ethics in the matter?" In every instance the failure of the clergy to reach a decision to act arose from their inability to find satisfactory answers to their own questions.

The problem eventually came to center in the political realm—on the moral right of the Church to adopt a plan with elements of political coercion in it. Up to this point the clergy had made to the elected officials only such proposals as they felt were based on their deepest spiritual convictions. They had quoted with approval President Eisenhower's words: "The founders of our nation clearly felt that free government is a political expression of religious faith." They had cited with special emphasis the phrase from the Prayer Book prayer for the President and all in civil authority: "Make them ever mindful of their calling to serve this people in thy fear." But the casualness with which those in elective office had received these recommendations proved to be occasions of increasing frustration to the clergy.

## THE CRISIS PRINCIPLE

Accordingly, the ministers felt called upon to advance a "crisis principle." While admitting the principle of separation of Church and State, they concluded, nevertheless, that *the Church had a responsibility to use every Christian and democratic means for directing and assisting a government in achieving its moral and spiritual goals.* At the same time it seemed proper to remind those in authority that government was only means to this end—never an end in itself.

The discussions of the clergy, preliminary to arriving at this "crisis principle," were exploratory and, for the most part, held privately by small groups. The proposals that grew out of these discussions did not, therefore, reach the floor of the Ministerial Alliance for action since questions about the element of coercion in the proposals were never fully resolved within the smaller groups.

The thinking that lay behind the adoption of this crisis principle in the minds of the clergy may be outlined as follows: It is necessary sometimes in a specific dispute to prepare the way for ultimate reconciliation by awakening in the antagonists a recognition of their need to resolve the disputed issues by moral means. The will-to-power in all men was noted and the fact that it does not lend itself to humble surrender; also noted was the temptation "to save face" even in the teeth of an inward acknowledgment of wrong doing. It was recognized that parties that have already made their "here I stand" do not readily arrive at terms of voluntary cooperation; indeed, even the explanations made from such a position, though made in all sincerity, must be suspect. There are, however, the immediate and pressing demands of justice, and since the seeds of love grow so slowly, the element of coercion becomes essential if the demands of justice are to be met —and, eventually, if those of love also.

The scriptural authority for this point of view lay in the fact that the Gospel of Christ is not only a Gospel of love: it is also a way of dealing with man's disobedience

115

to that love. The argument was advanced that sinful man can no more work out his social salvation apart from God than he can obtain his personal one. His thirst for power in seeking his own ends will quence itself at the cost of the individual rights of others and of the great democratic principles of liberty, justice, and equality unless there is some common plane where Church and State can meet. Therefore, it was contended that Christianity had a real responsibility to exercise a political force on political issues, not only as a preventive against ambition in high places, but also as a rein which would guide government in a direction more closely approximating that demanded by the Kingdom of God upon earth.

This, then, was the theoretical basis for the crisis principle. The question, however, of how to apply it in the present crisis brought the deliberations of the clergy to a standstill. There was, of course, at no time any consideration given to an actual political campaign with a slate of candidates, speakers, promises, handbills and a downtown headquarters—these techniques were too preposterous to be considered. What was considered, however, was a series of proposals designed to make the political authorities realize that Christianity is a power to be reckoned with. The search was made for a way of showing that an election booth can be transformed into a house of prayer, and a ballot box into an alms bason, offering Christian convictions to God. Regretfully, no ready answers were forthcoming, but the proposals following did receive thoughtful consideration and may be worth the consideration of the Church at large.

## THREE PROPOSALS

First of all, there was the proposal for the issuance of a "Little Rock Manifesto" similar to that issued by the eighty clergymen of Atlanta, Georgia. It was felt that such a proclamation could serve the dual purpose of stating the Christian position and indicating the powerful unanimity of its many signers. It was not inconceivable that each signer of the Manifesto would have a following both in his congregation and the community. Such a proposal might also win other supporters, and together, these would represent an imposing number of votes.

When the Atlanta ministers made their declaration, a local newspaper editorialized: "Yesterday eighty Atlantians, each one a minister of the Gospel, spoke out frankly on the critical problem in human relations which confronts our generation. . . . They began with an obligation to speak their convictions which are moral and spiritual as well as political. . . . A Southland and a nation will listen with respect."

A Little Rock manifesto is still planned, and it is hoped that it will claim similar community support, and will influence political leaders as an expression of the will of the people. The emphasis of this manifesto, however, will be upon the Christian statement and not upon political implications.

This proposal also included a suggestion for the issuance of a study guide for the churches. In 1954 the Department of Christian Social Relations in the Episcopal Diocese of Mississippi had prepared such a pamphlet which proved successful as an educational medium. Issued under the

117

title, "The Church Considers the Supreme Court Decision," it reminded the reader that the Constitution and the Declaration of Independence were documents which re-affirmed the biblical doctrine of the dignity and worth of the individual. It explained further that religion lies at the heart of democracy and political action can be a device for proclaiming faith—a consideration that President Eisenhower had also mentioned in his letter.

Admitting the difficulties which always lie between the proclamation of a principle and its practicable application, the Guide made four specific recommendations for Christians to carry out:

1. It called upon both races to pull down the barriers of antagonism and re-open communications.
2. It asked white people to recognize the importance of working with representative Negro leaders in finding a solution to desegregation.
3. It besought parents to protect their children from prejudice and ill will towards members of the other race.
4. It called upon Episcopal congregations to open their services of worship to any churchman without regard for race or color.

The brochure concluded with the following challenge:

"Times of crises are times for greatness. Man is at his best—or at his worst—under such conditions. Crisis builds character and makes men, but it can also destroy the fearful and faint of heart. Our job is to make the decision for greatness at this moment in history and pray to God that He may give us the strength to be faithful to do His will."

It was believed such a pamphlet might serve both an instructive and persuasive purpose in Little Rock. Prepared under the auspices of the Ministerial Alliance and distributed not only among the congregations, but personally to the leaders of the various factions by strong representative committees of clergy and laymen, it seemed to offer the basis both for the discussion groups planned by the Ministry of Reconciliation and at the same time for the exertion of a moral pressure upon the civil authorities. However, the plan had to be rejected for want of time. Events in Little Rock moved too rapidly for any study guide to keep up with them. It might have been helpful to have issued such a brochure or pamphlet several years previously—now it was considered too late.

The second proposal called for the framing and circulation of petitions. This was considered as a more forceful way of permitting moderate citizens to be counted than the Day of Prayer had been, and a better means of bringing pressure to bear upon the political leadership. It was thought that a handful of convinced and determined people could and should assume the responsibility for obtaining the signatures of the moderate Little Rock citizens. The C.C.C. was organized to work in this way and had been sending their volunteers from store to store in downtown Little Rock, asking the owners, with an implied threat of boycott, to sign proclamations against "mongrelization" and "racemixing." It seemed important to balance their activity and to arouse the moderates to the fact that their stand had to be witnessed.

Since October 12, moderate citizens have begun to

come forward and offer assistance. But at the beginning a spirited general action was greatly needed. People regularly expressed the hope that someone would step forth and lead. They felt the need for such leadership. However, they made little effort to seek a leader or to urge one to come forward. Was initiative and coercion also required here? Was it the task of the Church to circulate such petitions, draw forth public sentiment, use it as a tool to break down barriers?

Again, there were those who believed that it was. The passing of several months had helped to calm passions and reduce fears, and the discussion groups had begun to exert some influence. The Ministry of Reconciliation was proving to be a slow process, however, and the threat of time running out was ever present. It continued to be a fact that people were concluding their group discussions in pessimism and frustration. There was also the problem of semantics and, consequently, of communication, even among people of similar persuasion. For instance, in one recent closed meeting, four well-known specialists—a lawyer, a clergyman, a sociologist, and an educator—formed a panel to discuss the findings of a newspaper editor. In quick succession each explained, "This is a judicial problem." "This is a moral problem." "This is a sociological problem." "This is an educational problem." And when each offered his solution, the others nodded agreeably, but with no real comprehension of his plan. Each in turn could not but feel isolated, misunderstood, and frustrated.

This situation was especially true of such public organizations as the luncheon clubs, the Parent Teachers Association and the Chamber of Commerce. There continued to

120

be a differing emphasis and approach on the part of those who agreed in principle, as well as a complete disagreement in principle on the part of many others. This made for a marked sense of aloneness—with all its power to inhibit— on the part of individuals and precluded the organizations from any role of leadership.

The large number of "newcomers" to Little Rock, who were leaders in other areas of community life felt, almost without exception, hesitant about taking any initiative on this question because of their short residence. Like most places in the South and Southwest, Little Rock is inclined to label anyone a "newcomer" whose parents had not been born here. The same remark is made, as is made in Virginia or Alabama or South Carolina, "They are newcomers. They do not understand Arkansas and Arkansas people." This attitude has been an almost insurmountable stumbling block to a large number of moderate people who otherwise would have helped.

There is also little doubt that the continuing threats of economic and social boycott, the anonymous telephone calls, the abusive letters and regular mailings of the aggressive segregationist group have contributed heavily to the default of leadership.

With the situation so complex, the lack of initiative on the part of private citizens was perhaps understandable. Yet the stern demands of immediate justice remained, and, because of these, the necessity that private citizens speak. This imperative lay behind the thinking of those who proposed the Petition Plan. But many church leaders had misgivings about the part the Church should play in the organization of such a program.

121

A final proposal raised the question about the role the students at Central High School might play in the controversy. The sons and daughters of members of the C.C.C. and the League of Central High School Mothers had been thoroughly indoctrinated by their parents in the role they should assume. There was a well organized system of harassment against the Negro students: insults, name calling, sly kicks and hidden shoves, slogans pencilled on the wall, and open threats. One Negro student and one white student have been expelled. When the Negro student was expelled, signs immediately began to appear about the school with the slogan, "One down—eight to go."

This campaign of abuse, conducted by a few misguided young people, was met with the unhappy silence of the vast majority of students, who felt placed under an edict to do nothing. Yet some church leaders and church young people alike thought that this campaign of harassment should have been counteracted by the independent campaign of the students of good will. Such a countercampaign would have had to be organized by the students themselves and carried on in a manner that would show the small minority of troublemakers that they were outnumbered and in danger of social ostracization. Such a campaign would prove that the majority were not consenting to harassment and were setting up their own affirmative program to confine the tactics of the aggressors. This, of course, would have been a form of coercion. But the possibility of this program being realized was great, for the real leaders of Central High School were not the children of segregationist parents, but the children of "moderate" parents. Personal interviews with some of these student leaders indicated not

122

only their willingness to accept this responsibility, but the confidence they had of being able to fulfill it.

In addition, the proposal included the possibility of a letter addressed to the President, the Governor, and the School Board in which they would make an appeal for guidance and for the freedom to do their part in the struggle. It was believed that such a letter, if signed by the president of the Student Council, captain of the football team, and the head of the honor society, would have an overwhelming appeal. The fresh approach of youth, it was hoped, would influence the leaders to meet on common ground and, for the students' sake, to strive to break the deadlock.

Other suggestions hinged on this latter proposal. For example, if the student letters were written to those in authority, television, radio, and press could be successfully utilized. Leading stage and screen personalities might be induced to visit the high school to address the student body on the issues at stake. And, in addressing the young people, the speakers could indirectly reach the parents and the leaders of the various factions as well.

In the eyes of a number of clergymen this approach generally appeared to have merit. Having discussed the proposal at length, the original small committee which had planned the program of the Ministry of Reconciliation authorized one of its members to present it to the School Board. Though not unmindful of some major weaknesses in it, they thought it had a modicum chance of success. The artificial atmosphere of Central High School was becoming increasingly unbearable, and systematic education was becoming practically impossible. So it was hoped that student participation might accomplish some restoration of discipline and establish the social pressure that would eventually make troops in the school unnecessary.

Superintendent Blossom and the School Board rejected the plan when presented, on the basis that it asked students to assume a responsibility that rightly belonged to adults and placed these young people in a public position where they would have to bear the brunt of segregationist harassment. Furthermore, it was pointed out that the plan could easily be interpreted as using the young people to pull chestnuts out of the fire for those who did not have the courage to do so themselves.

It is probably true that these students would have been the target of some abuse; and that the plan could have been construed as calling upon young people to save a situation that adults could not solve; that it could have been criticized as making "tools" out of Little Rock's sons and daughters. The element of coercion was also involved, for force is still force—whether moral, social or physical. But in the final analysis, the proposal had to stand or fall on whether the students were being used as "tools" to save adults from their folly and as means in the broader campaign to open the door to mediation, understanding, and reconciliation.

Some senior students stated without qualification that they wanted the issues defined and explained. They felt they should have a part in determining what the solution should be, since it was they who were primarily concerned and involved. Those interviewed agreed generally that they could handle any problems of discipline if steps were taken to keep segregationist parents from gathering outside the

124

school. They were also well aware that it was they who were the inheritors of the future and that it was their education which was being so seriously handicapped.

## LATER DEVELOPMENTS
## AT CENTRAL HIGH SCHOOL

The indications were that less than a hundred of the nearly two thousand students enrolled at Central High School created the conditions which came to exist within the building. Some surveys indicated that there are probably not more than forty such young people—and perhaps as few as eighteen. The students, as a whole, were assuredly not thorough-going desegregationists, but they were willing, at least, to accept Negro students without retaliation and even, in many cases, to include them in their normal school life. Yet one twentieth, or less, of the student body seemed to have its hands on the temperature control. And since the last School Board petition, there has been a lessening of tension, but immediately prior to it, there was a series of bomb scares resulting from the usual anonymous calls to the newspapers, the School Board office, and even the police. Large firecrackers and dynamite without caps were found in vacant lockers. A hand grenade was discovered under the front porch of a nearby residence. There was an increase in the tempo of harassment and, if anything, the tension within the school itself increased rather than abated. Reliable information reported that the handful of National Guardsmen stationed in the corridors were still active in observing, reporting and, where necessary, interfering in the program of abuse in order to protect the Negro students. Meanwhile, any case of a suspension for dis-

125

ciplinary reasons by school officials was still followed immediately by legal suits and vitriolic name calling. The handful of aggressive students became increasingly bolder toward schoolmates and teachers alike. The other students were resentful of the ability of "these hoods to get away with it." However, the opinion became widespread that the matter had reached the point where the school officials themselves should take over the discipline within the school.

This is the picture which moved some of the Little Rock clergy to think in terms of a "coercion by youth." It seemed to them that the students might prove more adept at handling the campus problem than their elders were. Quite possibly these clergymen were wrong. Perhaps the parents of these students would have forbidden their participation because of the personal risk involved. Then, also, was the danger of the program becoming so artificial that these students would be playing the part of puppets to adult decision. In any case, the proposal was rejected, not only for lack of official sanction, not only because of the other problems raised, but because the ministers were incapable of answering the inevitable question, "Is this the Church's task?"

### HAS TIME BEEN SQUANDERED?

Whether rightly or wrongly, each of the foregoing suggestions has so far gone by default. No real political pressure has been exerted on the elected representatives of the community. Manifestoes and study guides designed to instruct and to guide the community are still unprepared. No petitions have been circulated and no calls made upon adult citizens or high school students to assume any initiative or leadership.

This tension between coercion and reconciliation is not easy to resolve. Though the pressure of Christian love has the undeniable power to change the world and the strength of Christian faith has indeed moved mountains and transformed kingdoms, there is still the demand that justice exacts of the present. At what point do love and faith forfeit their right to time? When does the Church have the responsibility to pick up the leather thong and drive selfish interests from the temple? And at what point does the use of coercion become a returning of evil for evil? The clergy of Little Rock have not yet found answers to these questions.

Meanwhile, the time originally requested by all factions as necessary for working out the desegregation problem has contributed solely to compounding it. Instead of affording the opportunity for breaking down barriers and reestablishing communications, it has been used to erect new lines of division and to bring forward more arguments for strengthening them. No mobs have gathered outside Central High School since September, but the organized resistance within the school increased to the point where the School Board finally had to admit its inability to solve the dilemma alone. At the cost of months and years of sacrificial endeavor, it has raised its hands in surrender and again petitioned for delay in the desegregation of the schools.

# 7

# BIGGER THAN
# LITTLE ROCK

In the issues that have confronted Little Rock, a single incident could become a tradition. The world has moved on, perhaps, to consideration of new items of interest. But the question is in order: Does it, in all seriousness, recognize the magnitude of what occurred in Arkansas' capital city or the full import of the issues still being fought? Seeds have been planted that could bear continuous fruit for the future. Tomorrow does not spring into being full grown—it is fashioned out of the facts and the acts of today.

## THE SOUTH

To the South, Little Rock has become the symbol of a national attack upon a sacred southern tradition. It interprets the Supreme Court action and the Federal military intervention as a threat to its future and a violation of its rights. Therefore, some of its people have reacted with a new Negro "phobia" and, in a few instances, counterattacked by proposing extreme measures. The pendulum of a clock never swings half-way—it completes the arc to the other side. In a like manner, the reactions of some Southerners have not been partial ones.

Before the controversial actions of Governor Faubus and President Eisenhower established specific rallying grounds for differing points of view, there was among Southerners—with the exception of the extremists—a somewhat academic approach to the segregation issue. This "wait and see" attitude did not require any action other than that being taken in the courts. The average Southerner was content to discuss the matter abstractly, but otherwise to depend upon legal training to defend his rights and traditions. He has been accused of "wishful thinking" and "whistling in the dark" by some of the more ardent segregationists, and of "blindness" and "a closed mind" by integrationists. Nevertheless, he has been content to continue *in statu quo*.

Now, the cry "Remember Little Rock" has become a call to battle. The academic question has been transformed into a practical one with strongly personal overtones, and what was formerly an intellectual exercise has become a matter of emotion and action. Both the mob gathered out-

129

side Central High School and the 101st Airborne Division sent to disperse it effected this transformation. If the "incident" had not occurred, it is likely that most Southerners would have remained quiescent, at least until some other incident occurred. But it happened in Little Rock. And while world interest may pass to other issues, this battle, so far as the South is concerned, is still joined.

One of the most alarming effects has been the campaign conducted by a few extremists, the techniques of which tend to remind one of those used in Germany in the 1930's. And a review of the two major theses of Adolf Hitler's *Mein Kampf* does not destroy this impression of similarity. Hitler believed absolutely, first, in the purity of Aryan blood; and, second, in the right to go to any length to uphold it.

"There is only one most sacred right," he said, "and this right is at the same time the most sacred obligation, namely: to see to it that the blood is preserved pure, so that by the preservation of the best human material a possibility is given for a more noble development of these human beings." [1] Hitler's attack against the Jews betrayed an uncanny knowledge of human sin as he played upon the emotions of his people. There could be no compromise, no middle way. "One can only succeed in winning the soul of a people if, apart from a positive fighting of one's own for one's own aims, one also destroys at the same time the supporter of the contrary." This was a refrain which he returned to over and over again. "The future of a movement is conditioned by the fanaticism, even more the

[1] Adolf Hitler, *Mein Kampf* (New York: Reynal & Hitchcock, 1939), p. 606. The quotations that follow are from pp. 468, 485, 786, and 468. Quoted with permission.

130

intolerance, with which its adherents present it as the only right one and enforce it in the face of other formations of a similar kind." He gave his movement a religious character too, and quoted proof-text with little concern for incongruity as he allied the spiritual with brute power. "[The Youth Movement] upheld the view that its idea can be represented spiritually, but that the protection of this representation has to be secured, if necessary, by means of physical power." And with a bitter scorn for all "moderates" he wrote: "He who would win the great masses must know the key which opens the door to their hearts. Its name is not objectivity, that is, weakness, but will power and strength."

Founded on pride and prejudice, the Nazi state sprang up to challenge the world. Appealing to these chief human vices, it called them virtues and gave them a "spiritual" goal to achieve. And because no "moderates" rose up in Germany to contest this false claim, misery and grief and death to millions was the consequence. Happily, there is little possibility of this kind of history repeating itself in the South. Yet, let it be admitted that, whether by design or not, there are some embryonic characteristics of Hitler's Nazism abroad in the land. This in itself is an issue which thinking men dare not overlook.

At the other extreme, a different problem arises resulting from the attitudes of the best intentioned. A great many Southerners are well aware of the fact that as the Negro goes, so goes the South. They realize the truth of St. Paul's statement concerning the Church: *The eye cannot say to the hand, I have no need of thee: or again the head to the feet, I have no need of you.* Consequently, they readily acknowledge the necessity of *forbearing one another, and forgiving each other,* as well as the wisdom of losing their lives to each other in order to gain them. Moreover, they have lived close enough to the Negro to understand the pathetic queries of Shylock ". . . I am a Jew, hath not a Jew eyes? Hath not a Jew hands, organs, dimensions, senses, affections, passions?" Their longtime association with Negroes has created a compassion that is unwilling to exploit and that extends beyond the selfishness of their own needs. They try to help. They are embarrassed by the economic insecurity, the ramshackle living quarters, the indifferent education, and the dreary existence these things produce, so they have striven at no small personal sacrifice, to upgrade Negro living conditions. The difficulty, however, is that they have been striving to change the individual while the system continues to produce such individuals. Meanwhile, they are pointed out as examples of the consideration the South gives to the Negro and as proof that, given time, the problem will work itself out.

At the same time, southern Negroes, including those not closely affiliated with the NAACP, have become increasingly restless and impatient over the limited success of the desegregation plan at Central High School. The younger Negroes feel their leaders have not moved forward rapidly enough since September, 1957. In some instances, there is a growing suspicion that these leaders are too cautious and too inclined to wait. A general dissatisfaction exists over the "turn the other cheek" program which requires passive acceptance of white harassment. In a few instances, there have even been expressed desires to form Negro harassment organizations to counterbalance the

132

indignities being heaped upon them. Because of this some Negro leaders are becoming perturbed. They see the possibility of these younger members of their race growing too impatient, and a time coming when, having lost faith in the guiding and restraining leadership of their mature teachers, they might strike back against the white harassers in a way that would have a disastrous effect upon all concerned. And again, this possibility is part of the repercussion of the Little Rock situation. Indeed sparks which fly from the friction here could still fall upon a ready tinder and light a conflagration that might consume the South.

Then there is the reaction to the Little Rock story that is expressing itself through legislative channels, a means which some Southerners are using. The state legislatures of Arkansas, Florida, Georgia, Mississippi and South Carolina have granted their Governors emergency powers to combat Federal enforcement of integration. Alabama, Arkansas, Florida, Mississippi, South Carolina, Tennessee, Virginia and Texas have placed legal restraints on organizations known to favor integration. Since 1954, 148 state laws relating to desegregation of public schools have been passed. Five states now permit their school systems to cease operation in the event they are forced to integrate. Three have permitted their schools to close if troops are used in the issue. Six have modified, or completely abolished, their school attendance laws. Eight states now permit assignment of pupils to schools outside their own districts in order to avoid integration. The constitutionality of these measures may be in question, and the South knows this. But it also knows there will have to be years of litigation before the decisions are finally approved or reversed. This is as the

South intends, for it is determined to protect itself against another Little Rock.

Such reactions throughout the South combine to prove that what has begun here is far from ended. It is much bigger than Little Rock. Indeed, C.C.C. members and the NAACP, moderates, jurors, legislators and educators, the well-intentioned and the patient, all know that the issue is much more than a local one. As the Rt. Rev. Henry Knox Sherrill, the Presiding Bishop of the Episcopal Church, said in a press interview: "The racial question is not a geographical question . . . it is a national problem."

## THE NATION

This is a fact which has not been understood everywhere. Many citizens in the North have come to regard the problem at Central High School as a symbol of the South's refusal to comply with those democratic principles set down in the Declaration of Independence and verified by the Federal Supreme Court. There has been a tendency on the part of the less thoughtful of them to stand in judgment upon Little Rock and upon Arkansas, without the realization that this is their problem, too. Concluding that such a crisis could not possibly occur in their own communities, their correspondence has implied that the people of Arkansas are violently different from the people of their own communities and that even the churches of Little Rock are sinfully indifferent to the moral law. Not only have their condemnations been defamatory in character, but their penalizing economic boycotts have resulted in a loss to Arkansas' economy of literally hundreds of orders. Protests were reduced to such a level that Little Rock college

134

students attending northern universities found it difficult to cash checks written on Little Rock banks.

Such extreme reactions were, of course, both temporary and unrepresentative, but they did grow out of a general failure to recognize that the citizens of Little Rock and Arkansas are not unlike those of any other city or state in the nation. But the chief failure of these persons has been the failure to understand the nation's involvement and the continuing repercussions which the "Little Rock situation" will have on the nation as a whole.

The circumstances which have pointed to the existence of a second-class citizenship in Arkansas and the South have also pointed to a similar state of things elsewhere. The apparent success of an enforced desegregation at Central High School has given encouragement to "second-class citizens" in other communities—and not always in the right way. The emotional tactics of some organizations have already begun to influence those in other parts of the nation who hate Negroes, and also, in increasing proportion, those who hate Jews, Roman Catholics, Protestants, or just plain "foreigners." In many such ways the occurrence at Little Rock is having its effect upon the rest of the land, and today's desperate need is for all the people to look toward the crisis here and say: ". . . any man's death diminishes me, because I am involved in mankind."

The problem of race is by no means confined to the question of Negro-white relationships in Little Rock and the South. In the Southwest it involves relations between whites, Mexicans, and Indians as well as Negroes. On the West coast the Orientals are the chief concern; and around New York City, the Puerto Ricans and Cubans. These racial minority groups have watched the Little Rock story with concerned attention and have reacted in a number of ways. In Brooklyn there has been a flare-up in juvenile delinquency, not a little of which was precipitated with the battlecry, "Remember Little Rock." According to the Police Commissioner, the recent interracial street fighting in Philadelphia has been due to the Little Rock disturbances. A band of self-styled "Little Rock Rebels" in Philadelphia, after entering by a window, attacked a Philadelphia Negro sitting peacefully at home. Meanwhile, in Westbury, New York, the character Nellie Forbush from Little Rock in *South Pacific* was greeted with such lusty boos from the audience that a near riot ensued.

In such ways the crisis at Little Rock has exerted its influence on the members of many minority groups and upon these other "incidents" which have been erupting across the Nation. This further points up the fact that here is a problem of national significance—not a local or regional dilemma. It cannot be solved on a hundred local fronts where, for the moment, a crisis may have arisen. The crises will come and go—but the problem remains. A *revolution is taking place in race relations throughout the land on the question of what constitutes the stature and dignity of man.* Democracy is involved, so is religion. The battle being waged is partly psychological, partly sociological, partly economic, and partly emotional. How is America to solve it?

The nation is often described as "a melting pot." The words inscribed on the Statue of Liberty inviting the world to "Give me your tired, your poor, your huddled masses yearning to breathe free," are employed as typical illustra-
136

tions of a free people's generosity. Citizens are proud of the principles involved in such a disregard for individual and group differences. And yet, as a people, they have not yet reached a conclusion as to whether such differences should be ignored, eliminated, or glorified. This failure has kept the nation off-balance, and America is going to have to choose whether its "melting pot" ideal is to be its opportunity or its liability.

There is no ready solution. The paradox which exists between liberty and equality is real. A liberty which permits an individual of great talent to compete against another of small talent will soon destroy equality. Yet any attempts to aid a person of lesser talent by some program of equality immediately destroys the liberty of the other. This is the paradox which has created the gap between the American dream of democracy and its actual realization, not only with respect to race relations but also with respect to national origins and religious creeds.

Such a crisis, therefore, as the one here in Little Rock cannot be considered as an isolated incident. Its implications go far beyond the immediate issue of whether a handful of Negro students should be permitted to attend Central High School. What is involved is the national predicament concerning a right way to deal with racial, national, and religious groups in the same society. Indeed, the matter is bigger than Little Rock.

### THE WORLD

In fact, Little Rock has become the symbol of a "white democracy" abroad. It has done no good to remind the world that racial tensions are far more dangerous in South

137

Africa, or that injustice is more rampant in China, or that discrimination is more intolerable in India. Ours is the nation which holds, as self-evident, the truth that "all men are created equal." Ours is the Constitution which offers equal rights to all men. And, rightly or wrongly, we are the nation to which the world has looked in the past as the best illustration of a people upholding liberty and justice for all. But the world also remembers that we are the nation which used the atom bomb in Asia. And we are the people who presently hold the additional threats of H-bombs and guided missiles.

Therefore, when the Little Rock issue broke out into violence the fact became one of tremendous importance to the entire world and, particularly, to Asia and South Africa. The *London Daily Mail* headlined, "Bayonets out in Little Rock." Moscow's *Pravda*, commenting upon Secretary Dulles' statement that United States foreign policy was based on moral and religious principles, said: "The reports and pictures from Little Rock show graphically that Dulles' precious morals are in fact bespattered with innocent blood." The *Times* of India approved President Eisenhower's use of Federal troops, but in Paris the walls of the U.S. Embassy were marked with "Vive Faubus." French headlines also announced the "Violent Anti-Black Explosion at Little Rock." While Italian papers told of "Violent Racial Demonstrations at Little Rock High."

In the midst of the crisis, two correspondents, Mr. Sang Soon Lee of the *Kyung Hyang Press* and Mr. Kim Yong Koo of the Korean *Times*, flew to Little Rock from Seoul. In discussing the implications of the Little Rock story, they were asked how the Red China and the Russian newspapers

138

were using the story. They announced that for the first time in their experience they found the communist propagandists reporting the news without any discoloration. It was not necessary, they explained, for the Communists to distort the picture—it was sufficiently bad not to need it.

The thinking of these two correspondents also seems representative of their people. Mr. Koo remarked, "Koreans do not like to see anyone pushed around. We have been pushed around a lot, and we don't like to see others pushed around. It makes us angry." Mr. Lee expressed the bewilderment of the Koreans when they received the North Korean news reports. "We could not believe it," he said, "And we did not know how to answer. We have seen Negro and white soldiers together in our country. There was no trouble between them. We could not understand how there could be anything like the trouble in Little Rock." Both newsmen declared that the communist press and radio were making point of the incident. "They did not discolor the news, but they read the Declaration of Independence over and over again and then used Little Rock to show that the United States does not have the rights and liberties it pretends to have."

Mr. Scott D. Hamilton, Jr., of Little Rock, was in India on a mountain climbing expedition when he received news of the racial discrimination dispute here at home. He has remarked that Asians, on learning that he was from Little Rock, would ask, "Does the United States really practice democracy as it tells us?" and, "Can we trust the statements of American foreign policy?" Officers of the Pakistan Army told him that vast millions of uncommitted Asians saw Little Rock as a contradiction of American overtures to win

139

the friendship of Asia's people. And, Mr. Hamilton reported, "Russia has been able to use Little Rock as a counterfoil to charges of Red brutality in Hungary."

The *Evening News* of Edinburgh, Scotland, published a poem which reads, in part:

> *Men who kick Negroes in the face*
> *Make me ashamed to own my race,*
> *And make me doubt if civilization*
> *Has ever reached a certain nation.*

Meanwhile, closer to home, the *Daily Sentinel-Review* of Ontario published headlines that "Turbulent Whites Gather at School," while the Ottawa papers used pictures with the caption "Negroes in Gun Battle at Little Rock."

Some correspondents, quite naturally, expressed approval of the part played by the churches, but all supported the fact that the United States has lost face in the world because of the Little Rock crisis. A letter from a friend in Johannesburg, addressed to Dr. Aubry Walton of the Little Rock First Methodist Church, said in part: "The Johannesburg morning paper ran a cartoon showing Uncle Sam with a black eye labeled 'Little Rock'. . . . I hope the response of the churches and the activities of other right-minded persons will receive something near the publicity which the original episode has." Another from Ankara, Turkey, said, "My wife and I are exceedingly proud that . . . our Church has the strength and initiative to start doing something constructive about this situation in Little Rock. You have no idea the way America's stock fell . . . even the educated people have looked askance at us." Officials of the State Department have confirmed all this unofficially, and admitted that the Little Rock crisis has done an incalcu-lable harm to the United States foreign policy.

Of course, the communist propaganda concentration immediately picked up the issue of "color." Knowing that the world's balance of power lies presently with the so-called "colored" people, it has made Little Rock the greatest propaganda weapon yet used in proof that ours is a "white democracy." Segregation, discrimination, jeering mobs, and physical violence have all been advanced to discredit the United States and deny the virtues in "the American way of life." And when supported by the ad-ditional propaganda that it was the whites who used the atom bomb, hold in readiness the H-bomb, and are pres-ently striving to perfect guided missiles, the Russian con-tention begins to have influence on the susceptible people of the East.

Our Christian missionaries in South Africa and Asia say there is only one program that can counteract and offset the communist line: the program of sincere humility and proven love. America's vulnerability cannot, they main-tain, be protected by Marshall Plans or treaties or reciprocal trade agreements—helpful as these approaches are. Neither can its historic documents concerning the rights and privileges to be accorded individuals in this democracy outweigh the contradictions of race riots and prejudices towards minorities in the minds of Asians, Africans, or the "colored" people of India. They make their judgments not upon what America *says* it is, but upon what it *shows* itself to be. Even the nation's present open-handed gen-erosity is not enough. It is too impersonal and the question of motive always remains. "Why does the United States

141

give us of its substance? For the Christian love of humanity or for its own protection?" For such reasons, one Marian Anderson with her obvious humility and love is a better argument for democracy than all the written protestations of virtue and the abstract stipulations for freedom that the nation can produce.

The great need today is for America to prove it has a heart. History has cast it in the role of world leadership. The acceptance of the responsibility of this leadership on the basis of duty alone is not enough. Cold duty to others can never counterbalance that which is obviously amiss at home. A stern sense of obligation cannot compensate for even one such incident as that in Little Rock. There is, consequently, no alternative to confession and repentance, to humility and love. What the world needs to know is that America *cares*.

The place for Americans to begin is with an honest recognition that neither as a race nor as a nation does any people possess the right to cry "We have Abraham for our father" or to lay claim to being "the chosen of God." In such direction lies isolation, selfishness and eventually destruction. The United States may well be chosen as an *instrument* of God in world leadership; but if so, responsibility must reach out to meet moral obligation, humility must attend policies, and love must accompany its deeds. For in the life of nations as in the life of men, it is not what is said with the lips that convinces, it is what is believed in the heart and practiced in life.

Here is a matter requiring individual action, not only in Little Rock, but throughout the nation. Diplomats can adorn their speeches with abstract words like "liberty," "equality," and "fraternity," but it will take Americans to show what the words really mean. Clergymen can talk of Reconciliation, but it will be necessary for the people in the pews to express their personal belief in it. In these days, citizens of the United States have an individual vocation to witness both to their patriotic and their religious belief and they can no longer leave the bearing of this witness to their representatives in either State or Church. The principles of democracy and creed depend, as they seldom have depended before, upon the willingness of private citizens to express, at home and abroad, their affectionate concern for all men with respect to their equality and their opportunity. In fact, it is not too much to say that the national security rests upon it. Meanwhile, it seems certain that it will be a long time before Sputniks and Explorers and Vanguards become more important than Little Rock in the minds of Asia and Africa and India.

## THE ONE FOUNDATION

For the Church, Little Rock has become a symbol of the power of human sin and of the impossibility of exorcising it by smug pronouncements or some tidy routine. Yet, it is also a symbol of crisis according to the Chinese interpretation of the word—that is, as constituting danger *plus* opportunity.

No major denomination has failed to speak on the Supreme Court decision regarding desegregation in the public schools. The Methodists said: "We call upon our people to affect these judgments in good faith, with brotherliness and patience. In doing this all racial groups must be willing to admit their imperfections and seek to

143

correct them." The Presbyterian Church, U.S.A., exclaimed: "We received with humility and thanksgiving the recent decisions of our Supreme Court, ruling that segregation is unconstitutional—with humility because action by our highest court was necessary to make effective that for which our Church has stood in principle; with thanksgiving because the decision has been rendered with wisdom and unanimity." The Episcopal Church explained that "the Court's ruling is more than a matter of law and order . . . it is also a matter of religious faith and democratic principles . . . the Court's decision is just, right and necessary." The Southern Baptist Convention declared: ". . . we recognize that this Supreme Court decision is in harmony with the constitutional guarantee of equal freedom to all citizens, and with Christian principles of equal justice and love for all men."

Nevertheless, while most churches have spoken in some such manner, Little Rock has proven to them that it is not enough. Written resolutions have not induced salvation or transformed society. The world has preferred to blame the clergy for the judgments the Gospel has levelled upon it. And when confronted by stern truths it has spoken scornfully of "church teachings" rather than acknowledge them to be the teachings of Christ himself. Such a flaw is not entirely the consequence of the world's sin. It is partly due to the imperfect manner in which the Church has defined its function in the world and to the hesitancy with which it has advanced its right to authority as against the prevalent opinion that all religion is a matter of individual opinion and personal taste. This is an issue far bigger than Little Rock.

144

The Church is the Body of Christ. It is his means for attacking the world and eventually winning it back to God. Its teachings are Christ's teachings, its judgments are his judgments, its promises are his promises, and it cannot permit a secular society to pretend that it is something different from the Lord it seeks to serve. Not only do its clergy vow to give fruitful diligence to doctrine and sacrament and the discipline of Christ, according to the command of God: the laity also make a vow to follow Jesus Christ as Lord and Saviour. Clergy and laity together compose a loyal band of disciples who refuse to conform to the world, but rather have sworn to change the world for the love of Christ. As Bishop F. R. Barry has said, "The Church is the one institution in society which exists mainly for the sake of those who do not belong to it." Therefore, it is mandatory for it to claim the authority given to it by its Lord and to exercise an uncompromising ministry in the world he came to save.

And yet, as the Little Rock crisis has proven, it is precisely in this area of authority that the Church has been checkmated by the world and by the divided loyalty of many of its own members. The burning issues of life are without number. Each vies for man's allegiance, and each offers the choice between a selfish interest and a high cause. In such fateful hours, man needs the commanding authority of the Gospel, firmly presented and unhesitatingly calling for allegiance. This is both the Church's function and its authority. Therefore, the dictum of the Lord God speaking through the mouth of Joshua must in these days continue to speak through the Church and confront man with the inescapable decision: *And if it seemed evil unto*

145

*you to serve the Lord, choose you this day whom ye will serve.*

This definition of church function and authority, of course, calls for a reconsideration of the Body of Christ in reference to the body politic. Again, Little Rock has confronted the Church with an issue which is broader than the inability of its Ministerial Alliance to deal effectively with elected officials. It is an issue involving the true purpose of human existence. *The world belongs to God. Man is created to live in communion and partnership with God. Apart from his Eternal Father, man's earthly existence can have no eternal meaning—but with God, he becomes a minister, a son, a joint heir with Christ; his true purpose is both to love and to serve God and his fellow man.* This is our true foundation. Anything less is unworthy of God's creation.

Yet, in contrast, ours is fast becoming what future generations might well call the post-Christian age. Social, economic and political tensions have grown beyond the power of any but the Church and the State to resolve. And if statesmen are not capable of rising above the temptations and pressures of petty entanglements, or of putting their trust in something greater than atomic power and world markets, then God's world could enter a new dark age.

The issue is a moral one and what has happened in Little Rock is only symptomatic. But the condition points up the fact that the Church must increase its concern for the State and increasingly exercise a responsibility which is authoritative without being authoritarian. All political issues have their moral implications. Every Christian voter

146

should recognize his responsibility to examine both the character and the purpose of campaigners for public office. And while the Church can never claim the right to designate *who* should receive the people's vote, it does have the right and the responsibility to point to the true meaning of human existence as it is inherent in every issue.

## THE WIDER MINISTRY OF RECONCILIATION

Regardless of the degree of the effectiveness of the Church locally, the Little Rock crisis reminds the Church at large of still another matter which is bigger than Little Rock. It is the need, not only to levy God's moral judgments, but also to witness to God's reconciliation. Men do not understand that the Church can render judgment in love. They have not learned that condemnation and affection can go hand in hand. In his everyday dealings in human relations he has been trained by his secular world to think of all criticism as destructive and every judgment as a threat. The fact that love can enter either, seems beyond his comprehension. Therefore, for his sake, as well as for the Gospel's truth, judgment must not be separated from reconciliation.

As God through Christ has taken the initiative in restoring the fellowship between himself and sinful, undeserving men; even so he has commissioned his followers to a similar Ministry of Reconciliation and called upon them to show others what they themselves have already experienced. Then, when they have understood that they are reconciled to God, they are able to tear down all the walls of strife and estrangement that exist between themselves and others. In this day the Church is not unknown

147

for its cries of denunciation, or its calls to reformation; but no matter how honest the loving intention may be, the approach is still considered a negative one by the world. What the world needs to understand is that the Church's Ministry of Reconciliation is not one of admonition, but of *restoration*. Its chief function is to follow the example of its Lord in offering forgiveness and calling upon men to forgive one another.

This need to understand is not only in the world, but in the Church itself. Regular church-goers also require teaching on this dual role of the Church to judge and to reconcile if they are to remain loyal to the Gospel when an issue arises which tempts them to dispute its claims. Perhaps American churches, in the Ministry of the Word, have been negligent in this respect. Too often the preaching and evangelical message has confined itself to the theme of "personal salvation," without stressing with equal emphasis the great biblical themes of corporate duty, love, and forgiveness. If this be so, preachers of the Word now face, in the situation we are discussing, a stern judgment of their ministry.

Should these observations seem to indicate too great an element of pessimism, let the Little Rock situation remind the Church that no matter how hopeless any given situation may appear, Christianity is always ultimately optimistic. This may indeed be a "bent world," but it is still God's world and his Holy Spirit hovers over it with infinite compassion, ready to guide, to empower and to redeem. It is in such knowledge that church leaders of this community have continued to press forward against a seemingly un-

148

breakable impasse and are still taking heart concerning the future.

The Church's Ministry of Prayer has, as always, been the sure foundation. Through it, God has consoled the sorrowful, strengthened the doubtful, and encouraged the fearful. By it he has bound together men of different persuasions and consolidated them into a common brotherhood. In it, he has inspired them to rise above personal views, to seek greater horizons. Because of it he has enlighted their minds and purified their hearts. Their faith has been strengthened, their brotherhood deepened, and their love extended. Bitterness has been overcome, objectivity achieved, and forgiveness offered.

Although it has not of itself solved the issue here, prayer has made many Little Rock citizens more certain of God than ever before and more confident that he will always perform his part in obtaining the solution. The fact of their own prayers, together with the knowledge of the prayers of others, has proven to be the greatest single spiritual stimulant in their attempt to come to grips with the prevalent tensions, prejudices, and impasses in their bewildering situation.

And so, thousands of citizens in this community would agree that of all of the many aspects here which are so much bigger than Little Rock, none is more vital than the Ministry of Prayer. It has proved to be the chief source of their ultimate optimism.

In summary, then, let the importance of the Little Rock crisis be noted by Christian people throughout the South,

149

the nation and the world. Let the Church, both laity and clergy alike, see in its crisis, not only the danger but also the opportunity. There is much in this age which moves the cynic to think it a festering, sour, cluttered-up, and not-worth-redeeming time. To this the Christian can never give consent. Ours is not a perfect world, but the degree of its perfection must depend finally upon our individual capacity to receive the grace of God. If we know where we have failed our Lord, there is always the opportunity to attune our ears to new sounds, open our eyes to wider visions, and our hearts in greater love. The issue in Little Rock is not the only, or even the greatest, issue of our day. But pointing as it does to the frailty of man, it can also point the way to his greatness:

> Rise up, O men of God!
> The Church for you doth wait:
> In her your weakness will be strength,
> And she will make you great!